Praises for
Be Bullish 101

"As an academic leader, it brings a smile to my face to see professionals like Ed going the extra mile by leveraging their corporate experience to write *Be Bullish 101*. I believe many college students will benefit from Ed's playbook, which offers a clear path forward with actionable insights for launching a successful career after graduation."

—Shane P. Martin, PhD
Provost, Seattle University

"For students, this "must-read" book is a significant first step toward attaining career readiness and developing abilities to transition successfully to the workplace. For parents, *Be Bullish 101* is a great gift for Career and Professional Development tool kit for your own children, family members, and friends."

—Lisa Piumetti-Farland
Executive Director of Strategic Alumni Engagement
Loyola Marymount University

"Having served as a faculty member and in senior career services roles at several universities, I find it refreshing to see practitioners from the corporate world doing their part to help shape the leaders of tomorrow. I applaud Ed for writing *Be Bullish 101* and sharing his valuable insights, tools, and stories that will support college students as they transition to the working world."

—Branden F. Grimmett
Vice Provost, Career & Professional Development
Emory College

BE BULLISH
101

SECOND EDITION

BE BULLISH
101

Make The Big Leap From
College To The Workplace

Edward L. Avila

BE BULLISH
BOOKS

Cover Design by: Marwan C. Harb
Author Photo: Kate Zotova of Pacifica Studios
Foreword by: Lisa Piumetti-Farland

ISBN: 979-8-9993796-2-7

Second Edition: September 2025
10 9 8 7 6 5 4 3 2

QUANTITY PURCHASES:

Schools, companies, professional groups, clubs, and
other organizations may qualify for special terms,
when ordering quantities of this title.
For information, email author at edward@bebullish.co.

Bullish (bool-ish) *adjective***:** hopeful or confident
that something or someone will be successful;
optimistic about the future of something or someone.[1]

Dedication

This book is dedicated to my wife, Mylene, and my son, Nicolas. Thank you for your support, presence, and for walking this life journey with me. I appreciate you allowing me to share my countless stories about what I love doing—and that's recruiting. You are my inspiration.

I learned from my mom at a very young age that if you want something in life, you must work hard for it and go after it. It takes action, perseverance, facing your fears, and stepping outside your comfort zone—but nothing worth having comes easily. Most importantly, no one will just hand it to you. Be bullish and go after it.

Yes, even now, as an adult, I still hear my mom's unsolicited advice echoing in my mind—and it continues to guide me. Thanks, Mom.

To the thousands of applicants, job seekers, and new hires I've had the privilege of meeting over the years—thank you for allowing me to be part of your career journey. I've learned more from you than you could ever imagine. With 30 years and counting of experience in recruitment, I'm honored to share my personal stories, knowledge, and insights in this book.

Table of Contents

Foreword

I have the great fortune of working at a university that offers so much to students from the first day they step foot on campus through their stages of life as alumni. Every year, I witness bright and enthusiastic college students entering the university full of excitement to embark on a new chapter of their lives that requires a significant amount of effort and success to reach. As students, they are gaining personal knowledge, developing self-awareness, and seeking higher learning. These students are focused and determined to succeed once they graduate from the university. However, many find themselves needing support to navigate career exploration and find purpose that leads to a successful post-graduation transition. The good news, there is help.

Every graduation class has challenges adjusting to the working world. Today's universities take a much greater responsibility to help students make this transition by getting involved as early as their first year. However, staff, administrators, or professors cannot do this alone. It takes a community to actively, meaningfully, and genuinely support our students' success.

As an Executive Director at Loyola Marymount University, I invite alumni industry leaders to come back and play an integral role in the academy, as they are uniquely positioned to be our partners. These invitations range from participating in career and professional development panels and programs, being featured for a fireside chat interview, serving as mentors, creating internships, and other opportunities such as hosting student group visits at their places of work and recruiting our students for entry and other level positions.

In my long tenure at the university, I have known Ed for over 30 years as a student, as an alumnus, as a professional, and as a parent. Over these years, when I needed a subject matter expert for my events to help students with networking, interviewing, or securing a job, Ed has become my go-to person and has never disappointed me.

When Ed shared his plans for writing this book with me, I was happy for him, but more importantly, I was so excited for the many students and parents who would benefit from reading it. Ed has never been shy about sharing his knowledge with others and has been grateful for the many mentors who have helped him on his professional journey. In his book, Ed provides an insider's perspective that equips students and their parents with valuable knowledge and practical strategies to thrive in the workforce. As a parent of my own two children, I see how they can learn, apply, and take advantage of Ed's insights, tips, and tools for their career paths.

For students, this "must-read" book is a significant first step toward attaining career readiness and developing abilities to transition successfully to the workplace. As you jump-start your professional career, these chapters act as a career compass for many to use as a reference and a guide. It is all about continuous learning, adapting, and growing—the job seekers' skills to navigate the challenges of an ever-changing future. For parents, this book is a great gift for the Career and Professional Development tool kit for your own children, family members, and friends.

As you prepare to move on from your college experience and embark upon the next stage of your life, let me leave you behind some words of advice: stay engaged, build confidence, be intentional, and be bullish as you take the big leap to advance your career in the dynamic world of work.

Onward!

Lisa Piumetti-Farland
Executive Director of Strategic Alumni Engagement
Loyola Marymount University

About Lisa Piumetti-Farland

Lisa Piumetti-Farland brought her spirit and talent to Loyola Marymount University as a recent alumna in 1987. While at LMU, she studied sociology and business and was deeply involved in campus life—as a campus tour guide, orientation leader, and an active member of Gryphon Circle and ASLMU.

Lisa has dedicated 33 years of service to the university, beginning in student affairs and undergraduate admission, where she spent a combined 15 years, including time as director of orientation. In 2003, she transitioned to University Advancement, where she currently serves as Executive Director.

Those who have worked with Lisa know her passion is unmistakable. She has an extraordinary gift for helping others reach their full potential and achieve success—offering encouragement, insight, and unwavering support to everyone she meets.

In her current role, Lisa leads an enthusiastic team committed to building lifelong relationships that connect alumni, parents, and students with each other and the LMU community—advancing the university's mission through meaningful connection and care. Over the years, she has served as a "road warrior" for admissions, a moderator for the Belles service organization, president of the Staff Senate, and a beloved presence in the LMU experience for generations of Lions.

Above all, Lisa's legacy is defined by the countless lives she's touched, the relationships she's nurtured, and the spirit of LMU she continues to embody every day.

Message From The Author

I assume you're reading this book because you're either figuring out where to start or looking for a better way to prepare for the job market. Congratulations—taking this first step means you're already ahead of the game.

This book was created for college students who want a practical, honest guide to support their career readiness journey. Since the first edition, I've heard from students, parents, and professionals alike. This Second Edition builds on that feedback, includes expanded examples, and reflects today's job market realities. Think of it as your personal career coach. I'll walk you through everything from exploring career options while in school to offering real-world advice from an employer's perspective on how to land your first job after graduation.

Whether you're just starting college, about to graduate, or navigating your first few years in the workplace, this book is meant to be your long-term companion. Inside, you'll find practical strategies, personal stories, and tools to increase your chances of getting hired—and thriving.

I've had the privilege of working with thousands of students, recent grads, and professionals over the past 30 years, and I've learned a lot along the way. My goal is to share those insights so you can confidently pursue your goals and transition successfully from campus to career.

Are you ready?

So, take a deep breath, lean in, and commit to owning your career journey from day zero—because the sooner you start, the further you'll go.

Introduction

Let me start by saying, I love what I do as a Talent Acquisition Executive. As someone who has worked in the recruitment industry for over three decades, I constantly expand my knowledge of emerging technologies, new career paths, and transferable skills across different industries. In the past, recruiting often involved local newspaper ads, mail communication, fax machines, and phone calls. However, the emergence of the internet has rendered these methods obsolete, providing employers with the ability to find qualified candidates in a matter of seconds through many new avenues. As a result, online job boards, company websites, and job searches have become more complex and intimidating during the recruitment process.

After all these years, I still get satisfaction when I'm able to help an organization find that rare "gem" in a competitive market. This individual possesses all the right skills, values, and experience that impact a business in a positive way, whether it is in sales, engineering, product, finance, or any other field. When an organization makes the right hire, a recruiter could make an immediate impact by helping it hire a talent that could increase its output, focus on efficiencies, or better serve its customers. A recruiter could help a business improve its bottom line by sourcing and attracting top talent who can add value to a company.

The Talent Acquisition profession has a unique aspect that motivates me to assist people in finding their next job that could potentially lead a person to a new career path, professional growth, or advancement. This role is centered around building long-lasting relationships. As a recruiter, I have the privilege of positively impacting someone's life on a daily basis.

Working as a Talent Acquisition Executive for various high-tech companies in Silicon Valley, I'm often asked by executives, managers, employees, or connections within my network who have children going to college, if I could meet and help them find an internship or their first job. Some have shared with me that they see their child struggling and they do not know how to help, or in some cases, they are not listening to the advice they are giving them.

As a parent of a college student myself, I understand the worries and anxieties parents have about their children's success, job prospects, and overall happiness in their future careers. After years of investing in their education, parents are eager to see their child become financially independent and begin their professional journey. They want to see their child step up—taking responsibility for education expenses, repaying student loans, or even moving out on their own.

Over the years, I've dedicated my time to volunteering at various universities and college career center outreach programs. These experiences have allowed me to work one-on-one with students, helping them with résumé writing, mock interviews, and job search strategies. What I've seen time and again is a troubling pattern: many students lack the practical skills, experience, and confidence needed to succeed in the job market. Some aren't sure how to translate their major into a viable career. Others are still figuring out which path to take.

While many of these students are just weeks away from earning their degree, they're still unclear on how to articulate their strengths or navigate the transition from college to career. Despite holding a diploma, too many are simply unprepared for the realities of today's competitive job market.

And this isn't just anecdotal.

According to a recent survey, 58% of business leaders believe recent graduates are ill-prepared to enter the workforce, and 50% of post-graduates surveyed said they wished they had learned how to manage their career readiness earlier.[2] even more concerning, 48% of employers report hesitancy in hiring entry-level candidates because of the time and investment required to ramp up new talent before they can contribute meaningfully.[3]

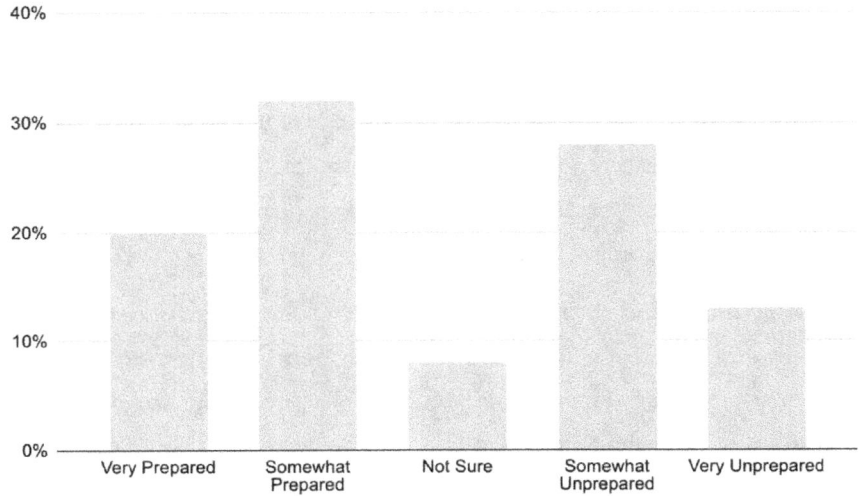

Table 0.1: Intelligent.com Survey Results

Table 0.1 illustrates a growing disconnect—between what students are learning in school and what employers actually expect on day one. And that disconnect?

This disconnect is more than inconvenient—it's a **BIG** issue with real consequences.

How To Use This Book

This book is designed to be your personal guide for mastering job search strategies, combining data, insights, and real-life stories into a comprehensive approach. Each chapter explores a specific aspect of the job search process, offering actionable advice and practical steps, such as **"Let's be bullish,"** to support you on your career journey. For the best results, I recommend reading the book from start to finish. However, if you already excel in certain areas, feel free to jump to the sections that best meet your immediate needs.

This book is divided into four main parts, each designed to serve as a playbook you can apply and learn from throughout your career journey. Whether you're just starting as a freshman or preparing for graduation, the strategies and advice provided are meant to guide you every step of the way. You'll find practical tips, real-life examples, and actionable steps to enhance your job search, build valuable connections, and develop the skills necessary for a successful professional career.

Here's the framework:

- **Part One:** *"Yeah, I've Got Time,"* emphasizes starting early in your college career to prepare for life after graduation.

- **Part Two:** *"You've Got a Friend in Me,"* highlights the support systems available to you, such as your university's career center and professors.

- **Part Three:** *"You Ain't So Bad,"* expands your knowledge to reduce stress and anxiety in your job search by breaking down internship planning, interview techniques, and LinkedIn optimization.

- **Part Four:** *"Why So Serious?"* deepens your understanding and equips you with further knowledge to boost confidence and enjoy the job hunting process, covering networking strategies, interview storytelling, and turning job rejections into learning experiences.

This book focuses on helping you stand out during Stage 1 of the Employee Life Cycle: Attraction & Recruitment (see **Figure 0.2**). Once you're in the door, other stages—like onboarding, development, and compensation—will shape your growth. But for now, let's focus on getting that first opportunity.

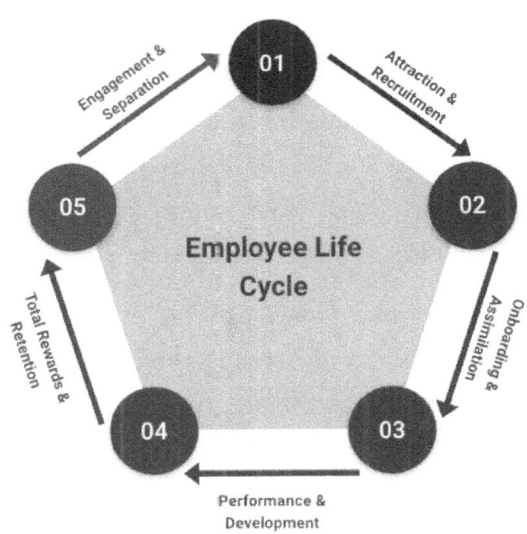

Figure 0.2: Typical Employee Lifecycle

In this 2nd Edition of *Be Bullish 101*, you'll also be introduced to the Bullish Career Canvas™—a one-page tool designed to help you organize your career strategy with clarity and purpose. Think of it as your personal blueprint to turn ideas into action and move from blurry to bullish.

By the end of this book, you'll have a comprehensive playbook that not only guides you through the job search process but also empowers you to take charge of your future, no matter where you are in your journey. I invite you to fully engage with the material, apply the strategies, and work towards your career goals.

At the time of writing this book, my son is a senior in college. Like many parents, I naturally worry about my child graduating and entering the "real world." Reading workforce statistics and reports about college students lacking the necessary skills for today's workplace can be daunting and, at times, terrifying. However, I started working with my son early in his freshman year to help him gain relevant work experience while in college.

We explored career options, identified the best methods for job searches based on his interests and strengths, and used many of the job search strategies covered in this book. As a result, he secured summer internships during his sophomore, junior, and senior years, gaining hands-on experience and job training to advance his career.

Fortunately, career readiness issues can be easily addressed through proactive planning, applying newly learned approaches, and taking charge of your future, no matter where you are in your professional journey. In other words, **it's time to be bullish**.

PART ONE

"YEAH, I'VE GOT TIME"

- Mr. Incredible

1

CHAPTER

WHAT IS THIS PLACE?

What if your college acceptance was just the beginning — not the final destination?

I'm a big believer in celebrating small wins, and getting into college is a major one. You should be proud of that achievement. But what comes next? College isn't just a place to attend classes—it's where you begin preparing for real life. It's your time to grow your skills, build confidence, and develop a plan for what happens after graduation.

Think back. Not too long ago, you were anxiously refreshing your application portal, waiting to see if your hard work had paid off. That waiting period? It's one of the most emotionally intense times in a student's life. For many, it marked the end of high school and the start of something new.

Now pause and remember what it took to get here: the late-night study sessions, SAT prep courses, application essays, long-shot schools, backup plans, and all the stress and self-doubt in between. You set goals, met deadlines, and pushed yourself. And guess what? YOU GOT IN.

That journey wasn't easy. You experienced a rollercoaster of emotions— and you came out on top. It took focus, commitment, and resilience. In other words, it was tough work. But you did it. Congratulations. Well done.

SANDRA'S STORY

In, But Unsure

Sandra, my colleague from work, was over the moon bursting with excitement when she shared with me that her daughter was accepted and got into her dream college. When she shared the news, there seemed to be a sigh of relief that all that she and her daughter endured was finally over. It was as if they had won the lottery.

"Ed, this is great news," Sandra would say as she continued to tell me every detail of her story. "We waited a long time for this." I was extremely happy for her as I knew how much anxiety and stress she felt during her daughter's college admission process - it was long.

When I asked Sandra what her daughter plans to major in, she responded, "I don't know." When I asked her what she wanted to do after graduation, she replied, "I don't know…maybe something in business, accounting, or something like that."

Sandra was ecstatic for her daughter, and I did not want to rain on Sandra's parade, but it was clear that their journey of trying to figure things out and making tough choices had just begun. They were days away from needing to make many critical decisions and other commitments beyond her daughter's college acceptance.

"College, what is this place?" you might ask yourself as you navigate choosing your classes, scheduling, and social life. Going to college is one of those major transition points in a young adult's life that will be remembered for a long time. It can be both exciting and liberating at the same time. Unlike high school, you begin to experience an overwhelming feeling of independence that most have never had before for the very first time.

In a recent survey of 366 first-year college students, the data revealed that 28% of students found Freshman Orientation helpful in preparing them for college because it allowed them to get familiar with their campus, understand expectations, and meet fellow students.[4] When asked what life skill they learned to use most starting as a freshman, the top responses were time management (28%), money management (21%), and stress management (13%).

During your first year of college, there's a lot to take in and learn as you adjust to a new way of life. Stepping onto campus for the first time can be a major transition, navigating the sometimes-awkward process of making new friends, familiarizing yourself with the campus, and understanding the university's language and customs, which can be confusing initially and may feel like an emotional rollercoaster.

CHANGING MY MAJOR - SHOULD I DO IT?

Like many first-year students, you might consider changing majors as you may not know what area of studies you want to pursue, and that's perfectly fine. Let's be honest: you can't be 100% sure if you'll enjoy the major you chose when you applied to college until you actually start taking the classes for it. It's all part of the self-discovery and personal growth experience that comes with college.[5] As college students embark on this path, it is not uncommon to change majors multiple times and explore other majors that may lead to careers that might be more appealing or better suited for you. In fact, 80% of college students will change their major at least once. Changing majors can offer an opportunity to gain clarity and realign academic expectations with future aspirations. This experience of this process allows you to make better informed decisions about your education and future career path.

Understandably, planning for an internship or even thinking about work after graduation is the last thing on your mind. Like many college students, when entering college, the goal is to enjoy your time and study. "Yeah, I've got time to worry about finding a job after graduation." Yes, that may be true, but you do not realize that time in college goes by quickly. So many things will happen to you, and it will feel like each year seems to blur into the next. Before you know it, college may be over in the blink of an eye.

CARLO'S STORY

When Confidence Meets Reality

I first met Carlo at a university career fair that I attended. He sported a backpack slung over his shoulder and proudly displayed fraternity letters on his shirt. With a firm handshake, he introduced himself, exuding a sense of unwavering confidence. He asked why I was here at his university as he was filling his bag with our company swag. I think he was simply strolling between classes and came over out of curiosity because he saw the quad area bustling with various companies. I told him we were recruiting for summer internships and entry-level roles. I asked him what his major was, and he replied, "Sociology" and that he was a freshman. I told him we are looking for rising juniors or seniors for our roles. After he took our company collateral, he continued on his merry way.

A few days later, I received a LinkedIn invite from Carlo. I accepted it, and then he followed up with a message asking if I would meet with him. I was impressed with his initiative and confidence and agreed to set up a time to chat. During our discussion, we had a few exchanges of pleasantries, but then Carlo dove right into the conversation and shared with me that he needed help understanding what he could do with his major. He contacted me because he was concerned that the career fair had no positions for Sociology majors.

When I asked why he selected his major, Carlos admitted that he did not give it much thought during the college application process, and his older sister recommended it. After taking a few classes in his first semester, he did not feel excited about it and wanted to know if he should change it.

We met several times, and I suggested what he could do before deciding to change his major. They were:

1) speak to his advisor or other professors in the department and learn about the possible career paths with his major;

2) connect with upper-level students with the same major and try to gain some insights from their experience or find out what they plan to do with their degree;

3) conduct a self-assessment of your skills, passions, and talents so you can align your major with your interests.

After some time, Carlo and I lost track of each other. Then one day, I got a LinkedIn message from him and discovered that after college, he pursued a career as a sales development representative at a software company, which he enjoyed. He stuck it out and stayed with the sociology program.

Like Carlo, it is expected to experience feelings of uncertainty –

"What am I really doing in college?"

"Is what I am majoring in what I want to do for the rest of my life?" or

"What can I do with this major after graduation?"

Questions about whether this is the right place for you or deciding to change majors can cause anxiety for college students. It's normal.

Your first year of college is challenging as you navigate changes. It's okay to take time to adjust. These decisions are unique to each student and a natural part of the college experience. Remember, you're not alone.

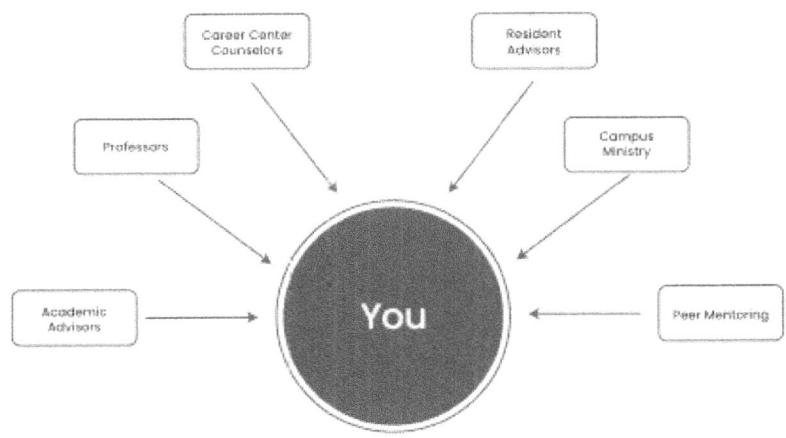

Figure 1.1: Typical resources available to college students

During your early years, your family and friends are the most meaningful relationships in your life, playing a vital role in your overall development.

Expectedly, your network will expand over time, especially when you start college, and you will be surprised by the number of resources available at your university (see **Figure 1.1**). During your first year of college, make it a point to connect and know them. They can provide insights and guidance that you would not get from your peers.

Begin to cultivate these relationships, as they will help you develop other aspects of yourself and enhance your overall college experience. They are available if you feel overwhelmed or need someone to talk to. These relationships are essential as they will allow you to expand your network (yes, your professional network), especially as it relates to your studies and career.

The best advice I got during my first year in college was to not panic. Take time to adjust to your new surroundings before making big decisions. Making decisions when stressed is difficult, so remember to breathe. Get involved in student activities and explore campus life. Whether you are an introvert or an extrovert, remember that you are not alone. You may experience anxiety or the "jitters," and it happens to anybody and everybody.[6] It takes time to get familiar and comfortable.

Learning to adjust to a new environment is an essential life skill and will be helpful in the near future when you start a new job. Consider this as practice when you join a new company.

Let's Recap!

- Starting college is one of life's biggest transitions—expect discomfort but know it's temporary.

- You're not alone. Everyone is adjusting in their own way, and that's perfectly normal.

- Lean into your school's resources early: professors, advisors, student groups—they're all part of your support system.

- Explore, get involved, and start to connect the dots between who you are and who you're becoming.

- Give yourself grace. Good decisions take time—and breathing room.

CHAPTER 1: WHAT IS THIS PLACE?

Key Takeaways

NOTES:_____

_____

_____

_____

_____

_____

_____

ACTIONS:_____

_____

_____

_____

_____

_____

_____

2

CHAPTER

THE FERRIS WHEEL

I often compare the college experience to riding a Ferris Wheel. Picture my childhood, filled with cherished memories of family trips to the Santa Cruz Beach Boardwalk in California, where our summer days were spent enjoying thrilling rides. One standout was the iconic Ferris Wheel. Its enormous, colorful presence always stirred excitement, though once seated and strapped in, panic often set in, prompting inner screams of *"Get me off this thing!"*.

Starting college might evoke similar feelings of anxiety or panic. However, once you find your stride, transitioning from high school senior to a college freshman, a new world opens up. Some days bring joy and excitement, feeling on top of the world, while others bring stress and anxiety.

Like on the Ferris Wheel, as it slowly rotated, I remember gradually opening my eyes as a young boy, feeling terrified and awestruck, especially at the breathtaking views from the top. Lost in the experience, the people below became tiny and then reappeared. After each ride, I hurriedly disembarked, eager for another turn.

Remaining on a Ferris Wheel for too long can become comfortable and predictable. If you only go to class and don't participate in other activities, college can feel repetitive and dull. You need to get off the Ferris Wheel to try other rides, you should engage with your campus community and explore new experiences to make the most of your college years.

Keep in mind, there's so much more to learn outside the classroom, and before you know it, the ride is over, and you graduate.

CATALINA'S STORY

Smart, But Stuck

I met Catalina, a senior and Communications major, during one of my office hours sessions at a local university where I was volunteering. She was well-spoken and articulate. After we introduced ourselves and settled in to start the session, she took her notebook and slid a white sheet of paper in front of me. When I looked at it, it was a copy of her transcripts with all her classes taken, and she proudly pointed out her high GPA. It was indeed impressive.

"How can I help you?" I asked. "I'd like help setting up my LinkedIn profile," she responded. When I asked her for a copy of her résumé, she said she did not have one. "I don't have any real work experience," she blurted out.

As with many students, I usually start by asking questions to peel back the onion. It is a process of uncovering relevant information by asking questions that allow me to remove each layer with the following: who, what, when, why, and how. I discovered that Catalina put 100% of her energy into her coursework and academics, and never engaged in any extracurricular activities or held a job outside of her studies.

Now that Catalina plans to graduate soon, she had trouble filling in the spaces on a résumé that's supposed to be the work experience. She signed up for the office hours as she found it difficult to know where to begin.

"Did I do this wrong? Is it too late?" she asked. I started to hear a bit of panic in her voice. "You need a job to get experience, but you also need experience to get a job," she continued. "Can you help me with this?" she urged.

Catalina and I did not waste any time as we jumped right in. We went through self-discovery exercises to gain insight into her four-year college experience. We deeply explored her courses, professors, class projects, and interests.

We had a few subsequent sessions over Zoom where we discussed her personal goals, passions, and career aspirations and spent time to align them to a potential career path. When unsure or having self-doubt about what she was thinking, she turned to her friends, family, and even professors for advice to get their perspective. What was once feelings of panic soon became feelings of excitement and enthusiasm.

Who knew there could have been more to Catalina's GPA, but yes, there was. It just took a bit of dedicated time to uncover her unique journey to gain clarity on her next steps.

As I start engagement sessions with college students like Catalina, I know I'm not working with seasoned professionals with years of experience or someone who has developed skills over time. From my first encounter with Catalina, I felt like she may have been on the Ferris wheel too long with no extracurricular activities. Career guidance has proved to be a catalyst in enabling a student's career exploration.

So, when I work with students, I start by asking open-ended questions to get insight into who I am speaking with. This allows me to probe until I have a solid understanding of the student. Here are a few questions I often ask:

- What do you like to do for fun (in your own time)?
- What do you consider your top skills?
- What would others say are your top attributes?
- What are your weaknesses?
- What is it about your major that excites you?
- What is your favorite class? Why?
- How do your family members (or friends) describe you?
- What are your favorite hobbies?
- In your free time, what do you like to do?
- Have you volunteered in your community?
- What is your dream job? Describe it.
- Who are your favorite role models?

Many students find it challenging to answer seemingly simple questions. Responses like "I don't know" or "Let me see" are common, but that's okay. I guide my students to think deeper for self-discovery, encouraging them to move beyond surface-level responses. This process may lead to soul-searching and self-awareness as they try to connect the dots, for some, this is a first-time experience. It is increasingly important to know yourself and what you can offer in a new position or career.

Steve Jobs once said, "You can't connect the dots looking forward; you can only connect them looking backward. So, you have to trust that the dots will somehow connect in your future."[7]

I have learned to use open-ended questions in a way that demonstrates one's self-awareness and progress toward professional goals. Self-awareness enables individuals to identify, articulate, and develop their interests, skills, strengths, and experiences relevant to their personal growth and professional success.[8] This may take a few sessions, but when you reflect on and identify your strengths, passions and strengths, it allows you to consider various career paths where you may excel and inspire you.

FINDING YOUR PASSION AND PURPOSE

You can't plan your career if you don't know who you are — but most people skip this step entirely.

There are countless assessment tools out there—Myers-Briggs, DISC, StrengthsFinder—that help you reflect on your personality, strengths, and work style. But these aren't just fun quizzes. They're decision-making aids that help you align your natural talents with real-world opportunities.

These tools are powerful because they help you uncover your strengths while showing you how to develop your skills and reach your full potential. Catalina, for example, started her journey by asking for honest feedback from the people who knew her best: friends, family, and professors.

Here's one tool you can use at any time to get a 360-degree view of yourself.

Areas	Friends	Professors	Parents	Me
Strengths	1. 2. 3.	1. 2. 3.	1. 2. 3.	1. 2. 3.
Weaknesses	1. 2. 3.	1. 2. 3.	1. 2. 3.	1. 2. 3.
Values	1. 2. 3.	1. 2. 3.	1. 2. 3.	1. 2. 3.
Skills	1. 2. 3.	1. 2. 3.	1. 2. 3.	1. 2. 3.

Career Scenario #1	Career Scenario #2

Figure 2.1: A template tool for 360-degree assessment

This tool enables you to gather feedback from close individuals who know you well and care about you. Here are examples of questions you can ask people who know you well:

- What insights does your best friend have about your interests, skills, personality, values, and strengths?

- How does it all look from your parent's perspective or your favorite high school teacher's point of view?

You will be surprised, often pleasantly, by the things others see in you that you simply cannot see in yourself.

The purpose of plotting the input on paper is to provide you with a well-rounded view of your skills and see them from diverse perspectives so you can home in on your strengths and growth areas. At the same time, you can identify possible career paths that align with your personal skills, interests, and values. You will soon learn that it is essential to understand

and highlight your transferable skills and interests when applying for work for the first time.

The feedback obtained from a 360-degree view can provide a much clearer perspective on exploring potential career roles, enhancing your current job performance, and achieving your career goals. By understanding the data on your soft skills and being aware of your own, you can identify areas for improvement, viewing them not as weaknesses but as opportunities for professional development. The next step is to actively seek ways to build these skills. Think of the 360-degree view to jumpstart your career success like Catalina, helping you take practical steps towards finding your ideal career with confidence.

Let's Recap!

- College is more than just classes—it's a ride filled with ups and downs, just like the Ferris Wheel.

- Take a step back to reflect on your personal values, interests, and strengths.

- Use feedback from others to develop a 360-degree view of yourself—it will help guide career decisions.

- Begin to articulate your transferable skills and where they can take you.

- Don't let the ride end without trying new things—get off the Ferris Wheel and explore other parts of campus life.

CHAPTER 2: THE FERRIS WHEEL

Key Takeaways

NOTES:_____

_____

_____

_____

_____

_____

_____

ACTIONS:_____

_____

_____

_____

_____

_____

3

CHAPTER

GET INVOLVED OR NOT?

Should I get involved in on-campus activities or not? Believe it or not, college students ask me this question quite often. Generally, I would respond to this question with a "it depends" on your preferences. Although I consider myself an introvert but social, I do not know if I am qualified to provide an absolute answer to this question for anyone "Catalina's Story" in the previous chapter, is a perfect example of a student who could find success without many extracurricular activities as she did not view it as essential for herself. However, it was a challenge to pull elements from her college experience to put into a unique story onto a résumé.

Most universities do a fantastic job of offering many extracurricular activities and diverse opportunities for involvement. In general, universities' mission is to develop and educate well-rounded students, meaning there's more to the college experience than the classroom. A recent study found that college graduates who were highly active in extracurricular activities and organizations were 1.8 times more engaged than their peers who were not active while in college.[9] This study suggests college graduates were more likely to be satisfied with their jobs, have a strong sense of purpose, and be involved in their communities.

It is not uncommon for universities to have over 100 student organizations for almost every interest. These student organizations exist to bring students together, help them acclimate to life at the university, connect them to other students, and help students develop transferable skills. Some of these are the following:

- Intramural Sports
- Greek Life
- Student Government
- Leadership
- Residence Life
- Political

- Academic Clubs
- Honor Societies
- Service/Philanthropy
- Multicultural
- Religious
- Publication/Newspaper

Whether you are starting your freshman or entering your senior year, getting involved in organizations at your university can have a significant impact on your overall college experience.[10] Clubs and organizations play a pivotal role in creating an exciting opportunity for you to join and find a community of shared passions where you can foster long-lasting relationships and enrich experiences outside the classroom setting.

If you're seeking to create a sense of belonging on campus, participating in organizations, or intramural sports teams can help you make friends, discover interests, or improve your interpersonal skills. If you're about to graduate, securing an on-campus job or a leadership position can allow you to develop new skills, enhance your résumé, or expand your professional network. Showing potential employers that you participated in, or (better yet, have led), a student organization, are transferrable skills that give potential employers a sense of what you bring to the role and what multiple responsibilities you're equipped to handle.

If there are no organizations of interest available on campus, then there is usually a process to start one of your own. The good news is that once you reach college, the choice is yours to do whatever you want to get involved in - there is something for everyone to enjoy.

MY STORY

Growth in Unexpected Places

When I was a sophomore at Loyola Marymount University, I learned about a program on campus called "Student Managers."

To join, students had to apply through the Student Activities Department. Selected applicants became one of five student managers, each responsible for operating a specific facility at the university. These facilities hosted a wide range of events, from small meetings and luncheons to live entertainment and conferences.

The student manager roles were extremely competitive and highly sought after. As a Political Science major, I was unsure whether I should apply. I lacked work experience and didn't even have a résumé. I knew I would be competing against upper-level students and those with similar roles in other campus departments, making this a long shot for me. But I thought, *"What the heck, you got this!"* I remember saying to myself.

So, I went through the interview process, which included a panel interview with five people and a 30-minute interview with the Director of Student Activities. It was highly nerve-racking and scary, but I knew that if I was going to have a chance, I needed to prepare well and do my homework.

I reached out to the outgoing student managers, who were all seniors, to learn about their experiences. I asked what they liked about the role and what they found most challenging. They shared valuable tips for applying to the program: just relax, be yourself, and be friendly. Using this information, I anticipated the interviewers' questions from the panel and answered them with a smile.

To my surprise, I ended up getting the role I was beyond excited and proud. I was selected to be the Student Manager of the Bird Nest, a popular facility overlooking the bluff with the best views of Los Angeles (see **Figure 3.1**).

Figure 3.1: The Bird Nest at Loyola Marymount University

Looking back, the decision to apply to the student manager program was a huge turning point in my early professional career because it gave me two years of hiring a staff, managing a budget, hosting student events, and interfacing with key administrators at the university.

Yes, I graduated from Loyola Marymount University with a Political Science degree, but I gained "hands on" skills that I could put on my résumé - who knew?

BACKWARD PLANNING

Let's be honest - college life can be a stressful time for many, and time management is a skill that you, as a student, will need to master quickly. With juggling so many things, such as meeting for group projects, attending classes, studying for exams, taking time to relax, and meeting friends, I'm amazed at how much students get done by multitasking. Sometimes, you'll find yourself wishing you had more time to tackle everything on your daily "to-do" list.

One thing that you may have learned directly or indirectly is the concept of "backward planning." You may have already been using this concept without knowing as you review the course syllabus for each of your classes. Typically, you look ahead for due dates or deadlines you will be responsible for during the semester. Then, you organize the necessary steps, working backward, to accomplish the required coursework.

This technique of planning backward and breaking down the various steps helps you allocate the required time for each phase, as it reduces stress, increases confidence, and leads to more achievable actions.[11] This will benefit and better prepare you for your end-of-semester assignments or final exams.

Backward planning is a strategy that can be applied to job hunting where you envision the end goal, in this case, your ideal job, as soon as you have graduated, and then you carefully plot the steps to get there. Once you have identified this, you can work backward to make decisions that align and prepare you on a path early. This knowledge of thinking ahead can help you make more informed decisions while still in college, allowing you to explore interest areas more focused.[12] For instance, where would you begin if your career goal is to work as a Data Analyst at a software company? By using the backward planning method, you might identify steps that would lead to a successful placement in reverse order, as illustrated in the following example:

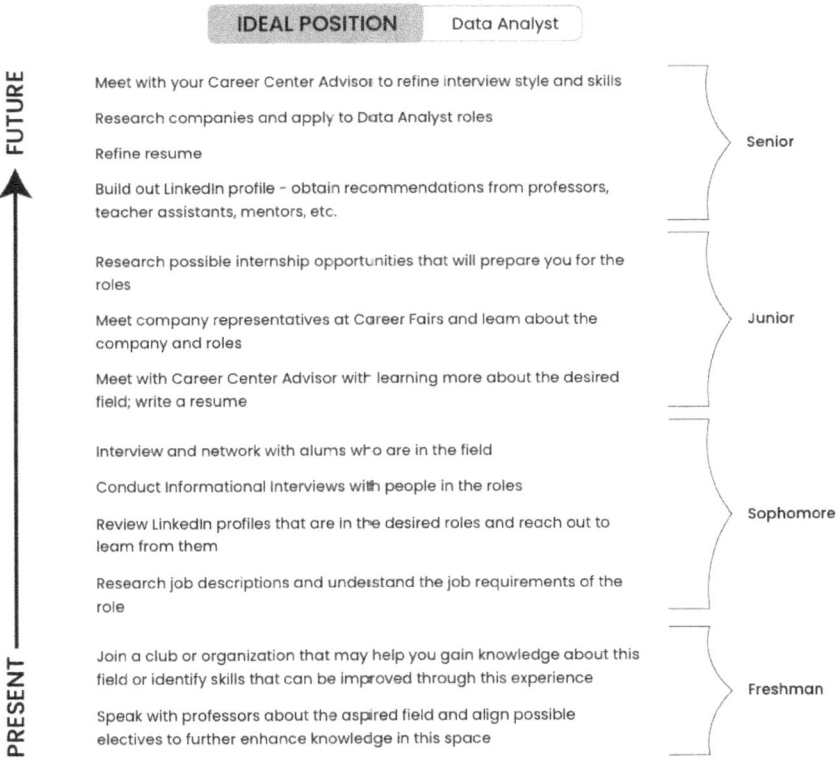

Figure 3.2: An Example of Backwards Planning

It's easy to drift through college without a plan — until senior year hits and you realize you're out of time.

Backward planning helps you avoid that panic moment. Instead of floating from semester to semester, you begin with a clear goal—like landing a data analyst role after graduation—and then work backward to figure out what steps are required to get there.

With this approach, every class, club, and internship become intentional. You're no longer just filling your schedule—you're building a path. You can start by meeting with professors, advisors, or mentors to outline the skills, experiences, and milestones needed for your target role. Then, map out a timeline that stretches from your freshman year to graduation.

This method, illustrated in **Figure 3.2**, gives you a clear roadmap and helps prevent you from feeling lost or overwhelmed. It acts as a "career compass," aligning your choices with the job you want—and making every move count.

🐃 Let's Be Bullish:

If you have already developed a 360-degree view of your skills, interests, and values, you're ahead of the game. By understanding the necessary skills to qualify for such a role, you can begin to align and develop them through your college coursework or campus extracurricular activities. This is where the value of participating in clubs and organizations comes into play.

If you still don't feel ready yet to outline a detailed career plan using **Figure 3.3** as a template, that's alright. We'll come back to it later as we continue to read on. With this knowledge, you'll slowly start to build out a better résumé through the experiences that you enjoy along the way throughout your college years.

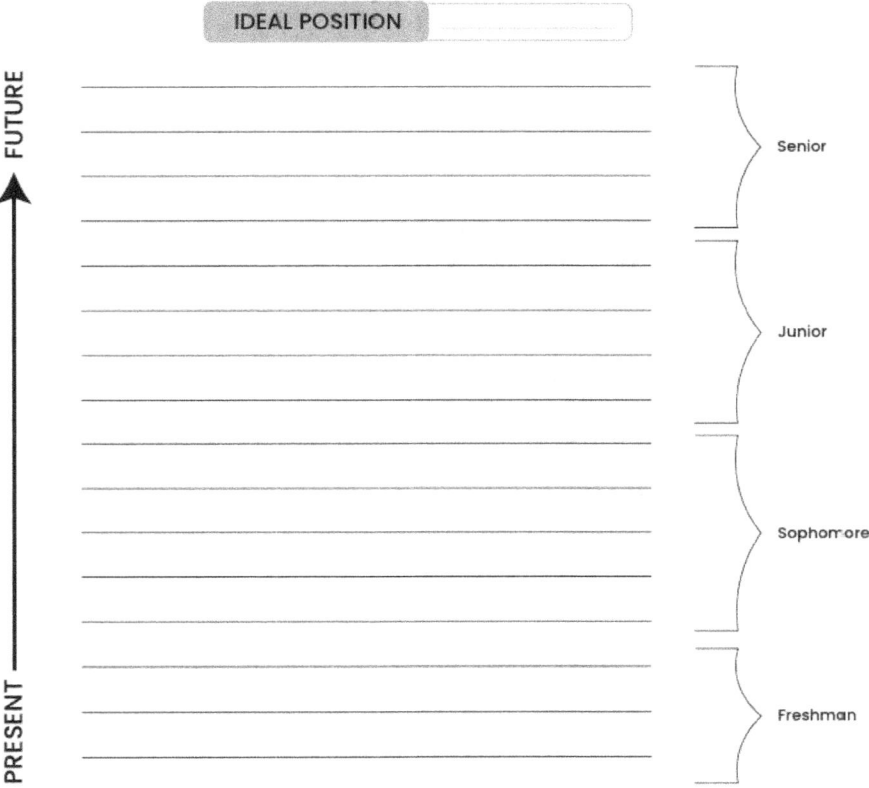

Figure 3.3: A Backwards Planning Template

Let's Recap!

- Beyond the classroom is where your real-world skills begin to take shape—join clubs, volunteer, experiment.

- Develop a working plan for the experiences you want to accumulate before graduation.

- Learn to backward-plan: break your long-term career goals into small, achievable steps.

- Use your college years to test, tweak, and gain confidence in your interests and abilities.

- Don't just be present—be active. Go where the action is.

CHAPTER 3: GET INVOLVED OR NOT?

Key Takeaways

NOTES:_____

_____

_____

_____

_____

_____

_____

ACTIONS:_____

_____

_____

_____

_____

_____

_____

Pause & Reflect

Before You Enter Part Two – The New World

You've started your career readiness journey. You've seen how employers think, how students often fall behind, and how the job search requires more than just a résumé and hope. You've also begun to understand the difference between waiting and *working* toward your future.

Take a moment to reflect:

- Have you built a clear picture of what you want—and what it takes to get there?

- Are you treating your job search like a process—or just a series of applications?

- Who are your early champions, mentors, or advisors?

Next up, we focus on relationships—because no one makes the leap alone.

PART TWO

"YOU'VE GOT A FRIEND IN ME"

- Randy Newman

4

CHAPTER

THE HIDDEN GEM

Most students don't realize their campus career center can be the key to unlocking real-world opportunities—until they're walking across the graduation stage with no job in hand.

Year after year, I'm approached by undergraduates looking for internships or recent grads searching for entry-level jobs. When I ask if they've connected with their campus career center, the answer is usually "no" or "not really." I always wish I heard more "yeses."

That's why I encourage every student to visit their career center and explore what's available. You may discover resources and opportunities you never knew existed. For many students, it becomes a turning point in their career journey.

Finding that first internship or job can feel overwhelming and emotionally draining—especially when you're new to the job search process. But you don't have to do it alone. Over the years, I've worked with many career centers across the country, and I genuinely believe they are the **hidden gems** of college campuses.

Think of the career center staff and volunteers as allies—like friends or mentors—who are there to help you prepare and succeed. They offer workshops, résumé and cover letter reviews, job fairs, internship listings, mock interviews, networking events, and one-on-one career counseling. These are not just optional perks—they're strategic tools designed to support you every step of the way.

Yet according to a recent survey, about one-third of students don't take advantage of these services at all.[13] That number feels low to me—but data is data. I understand college life is busy, and it's easy to overlook resources that aren't required. But here's the thing: these services are not only helpful—they're **free**. Yes, free. That's what surprises me the most. These resources are sitting right there, ready to be used, yet far too many students walk past them. It's one of the biggest missed opportunities I see during the college-to-career transition.

MY STORY

A Career Center Angel

I graduated from Loyola Marymount University in 1991 when the U.S. was in a deep recession, the Gulf War was taking a heavy toll on the economy, and unemployment was close to 8%. Despite these macro-level circumstances, one person was instrumental in helping me make a smooth transition from college to the workplace. Her name was Bernice Russell, and she was the then Director of the Career Center at Loyola Marymount University.

My first interaction with Bernice was during my sophomore year. I would see her walk around campus with other students or at various events. You can easily notice her among the crowd as she had a distinct presence and a walk with a quiet confidence as she strolled through campus. She often stopped and talked to students as she walked from building to building. One day, she stopped me in my tracks and introduced herself. *"Hello, I'm Bernice."* She asked me, *"What's your name?"* That's how we formally met.

We began meeting more often on campus and getting to know each other better. Bernice would invite me to visit her office and learn about the career center programs they offered. Initially, I didn't pay much attention to her invitation since I had no idea what I wanted to do after graduation and wasn't even thinking about it. My main focus was on my classes or the upcoming social events for the weekend.

Then, one day, I found myself next to the career center office on campus. I decided to drop by Bernice's office to say *"hello"* and a few exchanges of pleasantries.

Soon after, Bernice and I met more often, and got to know each other better during our one-on-one sessions. She encouraged me to attend networking events and develop new skills by getting involved in on-campus student organizations.

Over time, Bernice helped me research companies, review my first résumé, prepare for my first interview, and find my first internship.

Entering the job market can be painstaking for any college student. With the assistance of your university career center, you can take charge and boost your confidence in the job search process, even during times of crisis. Career center professionals can act like your very own personal career coach. They are very dedicated to offering much, from individual career counseling to hosting career workshops. They have the expertise to help you navigate overwhelming challenges and support you in pursuing your preferred career path upon graduation.

If you do not believe me, here are some tips and resources to explore so you can make the most of your university career center services.

START EARLY

First-year students may think it is too early to worry about their careers if they are not in their senior year. However, the career center is there to help you at all stages of your college life, including post-graduation. Like my experience with Bernice, a career counselor can advise you on what to do after your studies and which route to follow to get you where you want to be. You do not have to be at the end of your studies or the tail-end of your senior year to be looking for a job. The earlier you get started on your future career - building your soft skills, researching companies, or exploring extracurricular activities- the more likely you will be on the right path.[14]

Deciding on a career path is like making any other decision - it is personal. Career centers usually have self-assessment tools and career assessment methodologies that will test or evaluate students in terms of their personalities, interests, values, and other factors that will come into play when deciding on an occupation or job. *What is important to you? What skills do you have, or do you need to develop? What do you enjoy doing?* You need to identify careers that are a good fit for you. Sound familiar?

Many college students make the mistake of only going to the career center once and expecting instant magic - it does not work that way. As much as career counselors want to help you be successful, they cannot do it for you. You must fully own your future by participating in and committing to the career planning process. Remember, it is your career that we are talking about. Take the time to do the work, and you will see progress against your goals. Get inspired! Use each day and each engagement as building blocks to help you lay your foundation for your career. It is all about getting started and embracing the journey of self-discovery, growth, and fulfillment.

PEER ADVISORS

Peer Advisors are students just like you who have been trained by career counselors and are volunteers (or sometimes paid) to help you with your professional development. They are enthusiastic students who are available to provide you with support, assistance, and guidance during your career exploration journey. They are there for you to give advice and can be your biggest cheerleader, encouraging, advocating, and uplifting you every step of the way. Peer Advisors are usually upper-classmen who have been in your shoes recently and have a knack for supporting their fellow students' career-related needs.

WORKSHOPS

Career centers typically offer an extensive calendar full of various workshops throughout the academic year ranging from résumé development to negotiation skills. These educational opportunities aid you in career planning, job exploration, and career readiness skills. These workshops are delivered by either career center staff members or industry professionals with expertise in a specific topic. Whether you are a freshman or a senior student, these career development topics can help you develop a strong foundation and prepare you for your future. Here are a few workshops that you might see offered at your university.

- Résumé Writing
- Presentation Skills
- Building Relationships and Networking

- Mock Interviews

- Search Tools for Internships and Jobs

- How to Leverage LinkedIn

- Interview Preparation

- Tips for Phone or Video Interviews

With the advancement of artificial intelligence (AI), many college students are discovering the emergence of ChatGPT or Gemini.[15] This AI tool can provide a range of resources and guidance to help you in their job search. They can answer questions and assist you with writing résumés, cover letters, or other work-related statements. AI tools are a great way to complement what the career center has to offer. For instance, you may want to start with ChatGPT or Gemini when crafting your résumé and then solicit help from your career center counselors or peer advisor for final edits and refinements.

CAREER FAIRS

Career centers typically organize multiple job fairs throughout the academic year, which can range from general events welcoming all majors to specialized networking opportunities tailored to specific fields. These events are an excellent way for students to meet and engage directly with employer representatives at your university. It's beneficial to focus on the companies participating in these events, as they actively seek talent from your university or have a history of hiring graduates. Career Fairs allow you to speak one-on-one with company representatives all in the same place. Often, these company representatives are alumni of your university - what better way to connect and learn from their experiences.

INDUSTRY MIXERS

Career centers frequently host mixers with industry partners and invite them to come onto campus professionally to meet students. These events are an excellent opportunity for you to connect with potential employers, expand your professional network, build relationships, or engage with practitioners in your field of interest. These mixers are usually attended by university administrators as well in large settings like conference rooms, gymnasiums, or an open quad. If you can attend a mixer event, remember to dress to impress and use this time to refine new skills, such as making small talk, building your confidence, or practicing your elevator pitch. You might enjoy yourself and meet your future employer.

NETWORKING EVENTS

Believe it or not, social networks existed in the real world long before the internet, Facebook, and even LinkedIn. Meeting people in person is vital to career growth and learning opportunities, so network and meet new people whenever possible. You can build connections with individuals who can help you learn new skills or make introductions. You never know who could offer you interesting and rewarding careers in the future. Don't forget when attending these events, to try to make a favorable impression and be the person that employers will remember when they are looking for someone to fill a position. Knowing the right people still makes a big difference and holds significant weight in today's job market when it comes to finding work.

Career centers can put college students in touch with relevant organizations. They may also know of upcoming career fairs and networking events where students can meet professionals in the field, they would like to work in. According to a study, 73% of participants reported that they secured a job because of someone they knew either making an introduction or hiring them directly, and 76% of respondents believe *"knowing the right people is important to getting ahead in life."*[6] Some great network contacts might include people they meet at these events, which could provide helpful career information, guidance, or advice.

Students often hesitate to network because they feel awkward asking for help, but it should be an integral part of any job search. Though college students might feel nervous when approaching a potential contact, remember that networking is a skill that develops with practice, so don't give up.

These career fairs, industry mixers, and networking events offer valuable opportunities for students to connect with alumni who can share tips and insights on building a career. Alumni are often eager to offer advice, support, and potentially even make introductions to hiring managers at their companies. You never know – these mixers could uncover exciting job opportunities through alumni connections!

MELINA'S STORY

The Guidance That Gives Back

Melina is a senior undergraduate student working as a Peer Career Advisor at a university on the East Coast. As she plans to graduate, she has found working as a Peer Career Advisor to be one of the most rewarding experiences of her four years in college. She has assisted students from diverse majors, but one standout moment was when she was working with a psychology student named Mycaela.

Mycaela was so focused and adamant about pursuing a career as a psychologist. However, she has never spoken to anyone currently working in the field, which created some doubt as she will be a rising junior soon.

"Peer Advisors are there for students even when they feel uncomfortable," Melina reflected. "I remember moving my chair next to her (Mycaela) with my laptop. We popped open LinkedIn and started to do some searches for profiles of professionals in this field," she recalled. They discovered an alumnus who had graduated five years earlier and now ran his own practice. After sending a connection request and a message, they were thrilled to receive an immediate response. "We both screamed, 'YESSS!' and high-fived each other," Melina recalled excitedly.

Melina was overjoyed for Mycaela. "It was the first time I experienced the magic of LinkedIn on the spot. I was jazzed that I made a connection for her." Despite graduating soon, Melina remains committed to supporting Mycaela. "I've learned so much from mentoring her, and she's had a profound impact on me personally and professionally."

ONE MORE THING....

Career centers typically sponsor workshops designed to help college students excel in job interviews, covering everything from appropriate attire to common questions. They often offer mock interview sessions, allowing students to practice and refine their interviewing skills. These mock interviews are invaluable for building confidence and reducing nervousness, ensuring students feel well-prepared for real job interviews.

Like Bernice Russell, career center professionals, counselors, and peer advisors share the goal of helping college students find a career path that leads to a successful and fulfilling future. It's worth exploring the additional resources they offer. For example, they might provide perks such as designing personal business cards, accessing platforms like Handshake, or taking professional photos for LinkedIn profiles. You won't know what the career center can offer until you ask—so don't hesitate to inquire about how they can assist you.

🐃 Let's Be Bullish:

Developing and executing a career plan can be intimidating, even if you think you are armed with information to help you through the process. A career center counselor can add that extra something and help this process by providing career planning guidance, job preparation services, or just another perspective. They can assist you in laying out key actions, discovering activities, and focusing on actions that will strategically shape your career goals.

By working closely with a career center counselor, you can refine your interests and goals and design a Career Readiness Action Plan (see **Figure 4.1**) that links your classroom learnings and workplace experiences.

Using a Career Readiness Action Plan like this document and filling out each section, you can break down each activity, areas of development, goals, and actions. This action plan is a personal framework that you can use as an opportunity to project manage and outline a road map for you to follow (there are many other tools available like this one...just Google it!).

This strategic planning tool will provide steps that you can take to identify developmental opportunities, close skills gaps, and prepare you for employment.

Topic Areas	Areas of Development	Goals	Actions
Resume Development & Critique	• Resume is too long • Font and layout looks too busy • Do I include my clubs and volunteer work	• Needs more ample white space • Make it more visually pleasing • Refine Professional Summary section • Review statements with varied action verbs	• Meet with Career Counselor • Share resume with Peer Advisor
Mock Interviews Workshop	• Tend to ramble with answering questions • Shift too much in chair - no distracting • Used too many filler words when speaking • Responses need to be cleaner and to the point	• Refine Elevator Pitch "why me" • Enhance confidence • Improve posture and eye contact • Create rhythm for answering questions • Minimize the use of "um's, "like" or "uh" • Manage time for final questions	• Meet with Peer Advisor • Video Recording • 1-on-1 Coaching
Engineering Alumni Networking Event	• Feel more comfortable approaching strangers • Need to listen more and speak less • Work on eye contact • Know what makes "me" valuable or interesting	• Refine 30 second elevator pitch • Start short conversations • Be more engaging • Don't stay in spot, move around the room • Make 3 new connections	• Remember one unique thing and send LinkedIn Invite • Nurture relationships
LinkedIn Profile Development	• Build out LinkedIn Profile • Work on headline • Add relevant experience	• Take a professional photo • Add group project link • Expand Education section	• Visit Career Center • Get feedback from Peer Advisor
Find Connections	• Think about past connections • Teacher Assistants • Mentors • Find recent graduates at targeted companies	• Ask for recommendations • Increase connections • Ask for Informational Interviews	• Refine general outgoing messages • Customize note messages

Figure 4.1: Example of Career Readiness Action Plan

Let's Recap!

- Career Centers are more than résumé fixers—they're strategic partners in your professional journey.

- Use their tools, workshops, and mock interviews to develop confidence and readiness.

- Build a Career Readiness Action Plan to connect your coursework to real-world career moves.

- The earlier you visit the career center, the better your game plan will be by junior or senior year.

- Don't go it alone. There's a whole team ready to help you be your best.

- The bottom line is Career Centers are here to help - just drop by and say "hello".

CHAPTER 4: THE HIDDEN GEM

Key Takeaways

NOTES:_____

_____

_____

_____

_____

_____

_____

ACTIONS:_____

_____

_____

_____

_____

_____

_____

5

CHAPTER

I'M NOT A TEACHER'S PET!

The biggest mistake college students make? Ignoring the very people who grade their papers and write the recommendation letters that open doors — your professors.

Too often, students see professors as gatekeepers of grades instead of as allies in their professional journey. But here's the truth: professors can be some of your most valuable career connections—if you engage with them early and sincerely.

Building strong relationships with faculty isn't about being the "teacher's pet." It's about creating a network of people who understand your goals, can speak to your work ethic, and may one day serve as your reference or advocate.

I've worked with students who never thought to ask for feedback, missed opportunities to collaborate on research, or avoided office hours altogether—only to realize too late that they needed a letter of recommendation, mentorship, or career advice.

Why is that?

Initially, I believed the challenge was simply overcoming social anxiety—meeting new people or figures of authority like professors can feel awkward at first. However, I've come to realize that students often avoid interacting with professors not because they're shy, but because they're afraid of how it looks. They don't want to be seen as "trying too hard," or be labeled a "teacher's pet" seeking favoritism. In some cases, students feel it would be a bother or worry that it might be a waste of the professor's time.

Believe it or not, very few students take advantage of the opportunity to seek help from their instructors. So, kudos to you if you are one of the students that do-- consider yourself one step ahead.[17]

If you're not one of those students, here's a little secret: college professors are just people like everyone else. And many professors appreciate students who use office hours to clarify lectures, ask for additional support, or show a genuine desire to better understand the material. Students often discover that seeking help from professors is not only useful—it's not nearly as intimidating as they expected.

That's why office hours exist. And they can be incredibly valuable, even for short 10–15-minute sessions. That's enough time to get advice on a challenge, ask follow-up questions, or get clarity on class expectations. You may walk in unsure, but you'll likely leave with more direction and confidence.

More importantly, these interactions can positively impact your performance not just in that class, but in your broader college experience. Studies have found a correlation between how often college professors meet with students and how well those students perform.[18] When students meet frequently with professors in positive interactions, they tend to feel more confident, more intellectually engaged—and often see a boost in their grades.

Here are a few specific advantages of connecting with professors and how to make the most of their office hours.

OVERCOMING OBSTACLES

Office hours can help you better grasp course material.

No one is an expert in every academic subject - we all need help from time to time. When there's something about a class you do not understand or something you'd like to practice in more depth, your professor can help explain it differently or walk through it slowly with you. They may point out some "trouble areas" for you in the material you are learning. As you enter these discussions with your professor, they'll often suggest new reading or study strategies for you to try. A one-on-one session with them means you will have plenty of time to get help and support.

Your professor will appreciate your effort in coming in for help, especially when you are struggling or confused about the class material. It makes it easier for them to help you learn whatever you may be having trouble with when you make the extra effort to connect during office hours It demonstrates that you care enough about the class and your grade. With that in mind, be tactful and do not wait until right before an exam to get help; it can be hectic during this time—visit your professor as soon as you think you need assistance.

BUILDING RELATIONSHIP

Office hours can help you get to know your professor better.

It is important to remember that college professors are people too. They have unique interests and talents and can be fascinating people to talk to as they had a unique journey that got them where they are.

Attending a professor's office hours conveys your interest not only in their class but also in them as an individual. Meeting with your professors to discuss their past work and accomplishments can be worthwhile. You may find inspiration or get ideas for your career.

MOTIVATION

Visiting your professor during office hours can give you the motivation you need to succeed.

If you find a particular class boring or not sufficiently challenging, a visit during office hours may benefit you. Doing so gives you time to talk to your professor more in-depth, which may increase your attention and focus. You may even find the class more interesting than you first thought.

Often, visiting your professor during office hours humanizes them for you, and gives you an opportunity to learn more about them as a person. When professors are passionate and motivated in what they do, which many are, you can see teaching is not just a job, but a mission. There is an infectious enthusiasm that comes from people that are like this, and it will inspire you to set your sights higher and push your boundaries further, ultimately giving you a newfound respect for them. More than likely, you will attend the next class session with a renewed invigoration.

PROFESSIONAL ADVICE

Meeting with your professor during office hours can provide you with access to opportunities.

If you are really interested in the same field that your professor is teaching, meeting with him or her during office hours to discuss research opportunities can be very valuable. Professors can discuss their research experiences, which can help guide you toward one that might work for you. A professor may even have existing research opportunities in his or her department that he or she could offer you as a way for you to get "hands-on" experience under a mentorship style of relationship.

Professors often have connections with people in the industry. They get to know the companies who hire their students because they often set up events through the department or career centers. Their connections can also open doors to companies; and likewise, they may hear about opportunities that aren't visible to you.

Visiting during office hours allows you to receive career advice.

You can use a professor's office hours as a chance to answer broader questions about entering their field or pursuing alternative career options. If a professor knows you are interested in their field and they hear of an internship opportunity, they may recommend it to you.

If you are looking for an internship in a specific field and know a professor in that field, then they may be able to guide you to potential opportunities. If a professor can speak to your strengths or the projects that you have delivered in class, they may be willing to provide you with a reference for future roles or provide a recommendation on LinkedIn. But remember, this is most likely to happen if you have already built a good relationship with your professor.

MY (LONG) STORY

The Silent Mentor

As an undergraduate student at Loyola Marymount University, I majored in Political Science. As I got through my sophomore year, I often looked ahead and asked the upper-level students for their advice on which upper elective classes to take and which ones I should avoid due to how difficult the coursework or how challenging the professors were to get a good grade. This insight helped me pick the recommended courses to take for my upcoming semesters.

I recall one upper elective class that every Political Science student struggled with. It was called "Marx and Marxism," taught by the famous Jesuit teacher that everyone knew on campus by the name of Fr. Robert Welch, S.J. Not only did he teach this class, but he served as the department chair of the Political Science Department. Fr. Welch was a towering figure in his early 60's. You often saw him wearing old jeans, a washed-out polo shirt, and worn-out Birkenstock sandals. He was a true intellect known for how passionately he taught this complex course.

Needless to say, I could not avoid it, and this class challenged me from the beginning. It was difficult for me to stay on top of my class work as this course consisted of lectures discussing the historical context of Marx's writings, his theories of socialism and revolution, and the interpretations that later theorists gave of Marx's work. I break out in a cold sweat just thinking about it.

After the first couple of weeks, I had already felt lost. My study group strongly encouraged me to stop by during Fr. Welch's office hours on campus, so I did. I remember sheepishly knocking on his door until I heard a voice say, "Come in." He sat behind a desk that was covered with scattered papers and was surrounded by stacks of books.

At first glance, Fr. Welch's office appeared cluttered and messy, but when I began to look closely at the details - he had old, signed baseball balls, a few wall plaques, and political campaign memorabilia from the 1960's. It was like walking into a historical museum. I did not know where to focus my eyes as I scanned over his small office full of cool items. I had never seen anything like this.

"What can I do for you, Avila?" Fr. Welch's voice brought me back to focus. Honestly, at the time, I was intimidated by being alone in his presence, yet I was still completely open and transparent with him. I shared that I was struggling in his class, to which he agreed, and I wanted to know what my options were if I dropped his class. I do not recall what happened next as Fr. Welch talked about his early days when he taught at St. Ignatius Preparatory in San Francisco, CA, which is a high school that I was familiar with as I attended a rival school called Bellarmine College Preparatory in San Jose, CA. I think he knew a bit of my background.

Fr. Welch continued, sharing a bit of his life during the 1960's, a time of political awareness and the civil rights movement. "Ok, Avila," he concluded. I'll see you back next week here at my office and see you in class." I left his office wondering what had happened. I went to his office to drop his class and left with a scheduled appointment for another session along with his expectation that I'd be in attendance to the next class. Although I was perplexed, I was also intrigued.

I spent more time with Fr. Welch during his office hours and during that time he helped me better understand the class material, and eventually, I felt like I was in a good place. He also began to express vulnerability and shared his points of view and personal stories when "Jack" and "Bobby" were alive. I realized that everything I learned in classes or read in books, Fr. Welch was the real deal—a walking book full of historical stories.

One day, during one of the sessions, Fr. Welch asked me if I was attending the Political Science Association BBQ event on campus and told me I should come out. "There will be free food," he added. Say no more, I'm there I said to myself, but I responded, "Yes, I plan to attend".

When I showed up, several students and professors from the Political Science Department gathered around grilled burgers and drinks. This was followed by a softball game, which I stayed to watch.

Out on the pitching mound was Fr. Welch, warming up like he was about to pitch Game 7 of a World Series game. I overheard from the other professors that he was a savvy pitcher, and he once coached baseball at St. Ignatius Preparatory during his glory days. Fr. Welch truly loved the game, even in a slow-pitch game. He had a mean curveball and floater when pitching. He did not allow anyone to hit the ball as he struck everyone out.

When it was my turn, I stepped up to home plate, hit the ball hard down the right field, and sprinted around the bases for a home run. The second time up, I smacked it down the left field for another home run. On my third turn, Fr. Welch threw a few fast curveballs to challenge me, but I managed to hit it again, reaching second base. I don't recall the final score, but after the game, Fr. Welch approached me and said, "Avila, good game."

Before the BBQ event ended, Fr. Welch invited me to a meet-and-greet reception with some Political Science professors and students. When he asked if I was interested, I replied, "Yeah, sure. Why not?" He added, "Good, but don't forget to wear a coat and tie."

I walked into the reception area and realized this was a fancy dinner event full of university administrators, professors, and students. There were many unfamiliar faces, and I distinctly recall the moment I realized this, as my stomach sank. My heart raced, and I felt a slight tremble as I imagined meeting new people, struggling to sustain conversations beyond 10 seconds, striving to appear composed and collected, all while concealing my anxiety.

The event was to listen to several prominent Democratic candidates who were either planning to run for office or already in the race, including Governor Jerry Brown, who was set to make a bid for the White House in 1992.[19] I felt out of place until I started talking to a tall gentleman who looked like a professor. I had never seen him on campus before. We engaged in small talk, and he introduced himself as John. He mentioned that he was from San Jose, which is also my hometown. He shared that he had graduated from the same high school I attended, creating a connection between us.

John asked me about my major and my career aspirations. I admitted that I didn't have a clear idea yet, but I expressed my interest in working for a politician to make a meaningful impact in helping local residents with important issues. He smiled. As John headed to the bar for another drink, I followed him, and we continued our conversation. He became my security blanket for the night, and I didn't want to be left alone in a room full of grey and blue suits.

Fr. Welch finally appeared and said to John, "So I see that you've met Avila. He's one of my students taking my Marxism class."

"Sorry that you have this man for a teacher," John replied. I did not know how to respond or if I should laugh, so I did.

At the conclusion of the event, John handed me a business card and suggested that I contact him when I returned to San Jose for the summer. He mentioned that he was seeking interns for his office, to which I enthusiastically agreed, shaking his hand in agreement. When I looked at his business card, I didn't realize that I had spent a considerable portion of the evening speaking to the Honorable John Vasconcellos, a member of the California State Senate and a longtime state politician.[20] When John walked away, Fr. Welch leaned and said, "Nice job, Avila."

I eventually passed Fr. Welch's class with a decent grade at the end of the semester. For the summer, I followed up and called John Vasconcellos' office in Silicon Valley. I completed a 10-week internship as a legislative clerk, conducting research, processing amendments, and writing briefs and reports. When I returned for the Fall semester, I shared the internship details with Fr. Welch, who was happy for me and asked that I write a reflection paper about the experience.

Another time, Fr. Welch invited me to an event hosted by the late Los Angeles Mayor Tom Bradley.[21] He handed me a piece of paper with the details, including an address and time. The event was a luncheon called "Youth Leaders for Tomorrow."

I attended the luncheon, an event full of local politicians, city officials, and college students. Many of these students were ASB presidents or student government members at various universities, such as UCLA, USC, and Pepperdine, to name a few. Looking around the ballroom, I wondered why Fr. Welch asked me to come here. I didn't know it then, but I was experiencing imposter syndrome symptoms and self-doubt about not belonging in the same room as these accomplished students. "I don't belong here," I thought to myself.

At the luncheon, I sat beside a lady who introduced herself as Councilmember Gloria Molina.[22] She was a charismatic and friendly woman who put me at ease. I told her I was a Political Science student at Loyola Marymount University. She mentioned that she knew a few professors at the school, including Mr. Fernando Guerra, a professor I had just had in the previous semester. We engaged in small talk throughout the luncheon. In the end, she gave me her business card and asked if I would be interested in getting involved in campaign work. I only knew a little about political campaigns, but I still agreed and shook hands with her.

A few days later, I called Gloria Molina's office, and a Policy Aide answered and quickly scheduled me to meet with her Chief of Staff, Alma Martinez. During the meeting with Alma, she told me that Gloria Molina wanted to run for election and target the Los Angeles County Board of Supervisors. She was looking for volunteers to help with the campaign. She shared Gloria's story and explained her passion. By the end of the meeting- I was in.

I volunteered for Gloria Molina's campaign, making phone calls, walking precincts, and knocking on neighborhood doors. We organized teams to reach out to as many voters as possible to get the word out about Gloria Molina's position on topics to solve. It was an exciting opportunity to speak out about the local issues that matter to the community. At the end of the election, Gloria won, becoming the first Latina elected to the Los Angeles Board of Supervisors.[23] The overall election, while waiting for the results, was a thrill. Again, I shared the campaign details with Fr. Welch. He was happy for me and asked me to write a reflection paper about the experience.

After graduating from Loyola Marymount University, I returned to my hometown with no job, which had me in panic mode. However, when I read a flier at my nearby branch library that Ron Gonzales, a member of the Santa Clara County Board of Supervisors, would host a community meeting, I immediately went into action mode.

In 1991, Ron Gonzales was considered an up-and-coming politician with huge potential to shape the future of local politics. He was described as a charismatic and engaging leader. This was my chance, I thought to myself. I remember attending and meeting Ron Gonzales in person as he laid out his vision of bringing BART from Fremont to San Jose. This was a project that he advocated for many years.

At the end of the community meeting, I approached Ron and introduced myself. After an exchange of pleasantries, I asked if he had any opportunities to join his district team. He did not say no, which was a plus, but instead of telling me yes, he asked that I send my résumé to his office. Fortunately, I came prepared and had one ready with me which I quickly gave to him. One of his Policy Aides gave me an office business card and said that someone from the office would call me if there was interest.

I received a call from Ron Gonzales' office within a week or two. It was Jude Barry, Ron's Chief of Staff. He asked me to come in for an interview. I was excited, and immediately called Bernice Russell, Director of the Career Center at Loyola Marymount University, and she gave me some last-minute interview tips.

When I came up to the Board of Supervisors offices on the 10th floor of the Santa Clara County building, I bumped into Ron Gonzales in the hallway. Ron greeted me with a vibrant smile, which honestly helped relax me a bit. We shook hands, and he said how nice it was to meet with me again. Afterward, I was escorted to the office, where I met

Jude Barry. Jude was an intense guy from the start. No pleasantries, no smile, no "can I offer you something to drink," no openers of any kind. He was a matter-of-fact type of guy and got straight to the interview when we sat down at the table. I was ready for it.

Jude fired off a series of rapid questions, as if testing my ability to stay composed under pressure. He started by pointing to a stack of résumés on his desk and asking, "With all these résumés, why should I hire you?" Despite not knowing the role, I answered confidently. Then he asked, "Why do you want to work here?" I provided another solid response. Finally, he questioned, "If I asked one of your professors to describe your work ethic, what would they say?" I nailed that answer too.

At the end of the interview, Jude asked for references, which I was prepared for. I pulled out my sheet of paper and gave him the names and contact numbers of Fr. Welch, John Vasconcellos, and Alma Martinez. I heard back from Ron's office within a week, and they extended the job. Yes, I got the job—a Junior Policy Analyst.

In my college years, my life seemed like a jumble of random dots without no clear direction. I was still figuring out my post-graduation plans with my newly acquired Political Science degree.

In Steve Jobs' Stanford Commencement Address in 2005, he made a point about trusting that you know where you are going. Only after you are there can you connect the dots. When I think about Steve Jobs' quote, I had never considered what got me to where I was and where I was going at that time. I had not yet considered the dots, let alone connected them. When I attended Loyola Marymount University, I was a first-generation college student who lacked the professional relationships to secure a job that my more affluent classmates enjoyed. Steve Jobs conveyed the significance of connecting the dots in our own lives.

The idea of connecting the dots in hindsight is a powerful reminder that every experience we go through, no matter how small or seemingly insignificant, contributes to our growth and understanding. The dots finally made sense as I reflected on my interactions with Fr. Welch. I now can see how he influenced and helped me gain the skills to pursue my career goals. Everything you are experiencing today, no matter how challenging it may seem, will one day make sense to you.

As Steve Jobs suggested, our lives are a series of dots and only when you look back can we trace the intricate lines that connect them. Trust the dots will someday connect. Believe that the dots will someday connect. This retrospective perspective challenges us to embrace our distinct experiences, learning from failures and successes because they all contribute to the bigger picture of our journey.

Similar to my relationship with Fr. Welch, your college professors have the unique ability to affect your academics and your future career. Many of them started their careers where you are now: as students. Countless educators also work in their fields and can offer valuable, real-world insights. While their professional journeys may differ, their experiences can help you learn about possible career options and maximize your education.

Spending 20 or 30 minutes with your college professor could unlock a massive opportunity for your future success. If the standard office hours do not work for your schedule, ask to make an appointment. No matter what, you'll stand out — and you might just get a mentor, a professional connection, or even a friend out of it.

Let's Recap!

- Most students overlook office hours—but they're one of the best ways to stand out and build meaningful relationships.

- Research shows students who engage with professors outside of class are more likely to succeed in college.

- Building authentic connections with instructors can open doors to internships, jobs, and career advice.

- Professors are part of your professional network—they're often well-connected and eager to support students they know and trust.

- Referrals and recommendations are more likely when you're seen as more than just a name on the roster—so don't be shy, raise your hand!

CHAPTER 5: I'M NOT A TEACHER'S PET

Key Takeaways

NOTES:_____

_____

_____

_____

_____

_____

_____

ACTIONS:_____

_____

_____

_____

_____

_____

_____

6

CHAPTER

THE BLACK HOLE, IS IT REAL?

If you've ever submitted dozens of applications and heard nothing back, you've probably started to believe in the myth of the "black hole." But what if that silence is actually a data point?

The job search "black hole" isn't a horror movie—but it might feel like one. It describes the dreaded experience job seekers face when they apply online and never hear anything in return. No rejection. No feedback. Just silence. It's one of the most frustrating and disheartening parts of job hunting.

Has this happened to you? If so, welcome—you've entered the **black hole**.

According to recent data, 79% of job seekers say that not hearing back from employers after applying is the most difficult part of using online job boards. And it's no wonder. It leaves you asking.[24]

Why is there no response?

What's happening behind the scenes after I apply?

Are those job postings even real?

Why do some roles vanish overnight?

Do I actually meet the qualifications?

Are recruiters even seeing my résumé?

So many questions—and very few answers. But after more than three decades leading Talent Acquisition across startups and large companies, I can share a perspective from the other side of the table.

Here's what you need to know: there is no one-size-fits-all hiring process. Each company or organization sources talent differently based on business structure, urgency, team needs, and budget timing. Whether a job opens up, gets filled, or vanishes altogether often has more to do with internal decisions than with your qualifications.

⌕AN INSIDER'S VIEW ⌕

When it comes to an open position, Talent Acquisition Partners (or "TA Partners") typically work closely with Corporate Finance, also known as Financial Planning and Analysis (FP&A) Analyst. FP&A roles are vital to an organization's financial health and business strategic initiatives. They support the business, and they partner with leaders to assess how solid the current state of the business is. With this understanding, they can determine how many employees are needed to achieve company goals. This process is called headcount planning.

FP&A provides input and guidance to business leaders on whether a position is budgeted for hire. By knowing how many employees you need to hire to do a specific job, you will be better able to identify the required employee skill sets and qualifications. Some of these positions are called "addition to headcount" or "backfills." To simplify, "additional to headcount" means future hires that are needed to meet the business's goals, and "backfills" are headcount that has already been accounted for on the company's payroll, but someone has left the organization that there is a need to look for a replacement hire to fill the role.

Once the approved hiring plan is known and communicated, the Talent Acquisition team can work with the organization to plan for the number of employees, contractors, and interns needed to be hired. Again, I'm simplifying this process so that you understand what happens in companies when figuring out which positions to recruit for. However, it doesn't end there; this is only the beginning.

TA Partners are the recruiters responsible for helping companies find, attract, and hire qualified talent. They work with hiring managers to determine the appropriate experience level, skills, qualifications, and role location. They sometimes work with other internal specialists, such as compensation, to agree on grade levels/bands, salary ranges, or equity. Ultimately, the Talent Acquisition team collaborates with key internal stakeholders to develop the proper hiring strategy. Once you reach this point, the assigned TA Partner has the green light to post the job description and can start to source qualified candidates.

A seasoned TA Partner does not rely 100% on applicants who only come through the career site into the applicant tracking system (ATS). Sorry, but it is the truth. TA Partners use multiple sources to fill a position. A role may be filled by candidates from several sources, such as the following:

- TA Partners may reach out to passive candidates within their network that they may have been nurturing over time and update them of the role.

- There may be referrals coming from internal employees' networks once it is known that a position has been opened.

- Internal employees may express interest in the opportunity as a means of their career development or career growth.

- There may be internal contractors (or interns) that have been working at the company for some time, and they may apply to the role with the hopes of being converted to a fulltime employee.

This is why you might not hear back from employers. TA Partners can leverage multiple avenues to source and fill open positions with the best possible candidates that they are able to find for the organization.

GINO'S STORY

Behind the Job Requisition

Gino is a Senior Talent Acquisition Partner for a SaaS company specializing in technical roles, with extensive experience in startup environments. "I really enjoy what I do, and it has taken me a long time to learn the various engineering roles that we hire for," Gino shared. "When I get an assigned requisition, I get excited and take it as a challenge to find the best candidate out there," he explained.

When Gino posts a new role for a "Front End Software" or "Full Stack Developer," he quickly receives over a hundred applications. Before his initial screening calls, he reviews the profiles to ensure they meet the minimum qualifications and are suitable for the role. "At times, I feel that candidates don't read the job description and just apply with the hope of being interviewed.

Many candidates apply for the same role multiple times, which wastes my time," Gino said. He also contacts candidates through LinkedIn

Recruiter to see if anyone he has previously spoken with might be interested in the position. Filling technical roles typically takes about 35 days, which is favorable for his metrics.

"I can't respond to every candidate who applies to one of my roles," Gino states. He relies on Greenhouse, their ATS, to manage communication through automated messages. Personally responding to every interested candidate would be too time-consuming. "I only respond to candidates who get deep into the interview process, even if they are not selected for the role, as they may be potential hires for other positions I work on in the future," he admits.

Like Gino, many TA Partners are measured on performance metrics such as req-fill time and quality of hire, regardless of where the candidate came from. With many candidates applying for online positions on various social platforms like the companies' career pages, LinkedIn, or Indeed, hiring managers and TA Partners simply do not have enough time to respond to every job seeker who applies for the position.

When using online tools to help boost your résumé or generative AI platforms that draft cover letters for you, you still need to apply for job postings. When you do, you must realize that your first entry point to a company is met with automation solutions instead of actual humans. You may receive a standard *"We've received your résumé and will be in touch shortly"* auto-response or you may get radio silence.

You may wonder whether your profile made it into the hiring manager's inbox or has entered the black hole. As you can see in **Figure 6.1**, companies have invested in many automation solutions to be more efficient and save time with their hiring processes. Tasks that TA Partners once performed are now being automated with various solutions, leading to much frustration for job seekers. These automated solutions may be viewed as gatekeepers between job seekers and hiring managers. These functions may include scanning résumés that were submitted online, parsing them into searchable data, and ranking candidates based on predefined criteria. These automated processes are viewed as essential as they enable employers to manage large volumes of applications efficiently. However, it also means that your résumé needs to meet specific requirements to pass through ATS to make it to the eyes of a TA Partner.

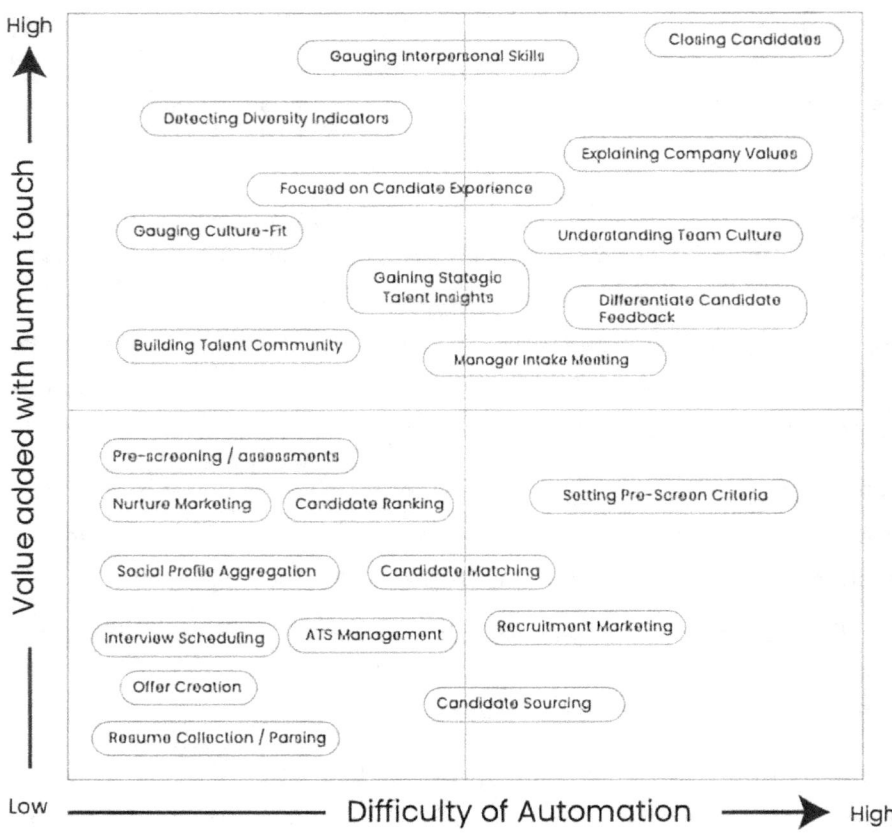

Table 6.1: Impact of Automation on Job Seekers

On average, for every job opening, an employer receives 118 applications, and only 20% of applicants receive interviews.[25] This number can surge to over 1,000 applications for each job opening, depending on the industry. Regardless of the number of applicants, you must know that the job market is competitive, even for internships and entry-level roles. Just sending your résumé alone into the mix of automated solutions seems like a massive waste of time and a recipe for disappointment.

These automated solutions have algorithms that look for specific keywords, and if your résumé or profile does not have them, you will not have a chance to speak to a human being. The goal is to use various job search approaches to penetrate and get access to the upper right-hand quadrant, as shown in **Figure 6.1**, so that TA Partners or hiring managers notice you.

Most companies today, including over 97% of Fortune 500 companies, rely on automation solutions to help them identify, source, and hire talent.[26] That means you, as a job seeker, should understand how to make your résumé stand out. How can you get through the automaton processes to connect with a person? That is the challenge. The more TA Partners lean on automation solutions, the more you need to know how the internal processes work. So, what can you do differently? Let me start by giving you an inside look at the behind-the-scenes recruitment process.

DATA-DRIVEN RECRUITING METRICS

Metrics are crucial in improving talent acquisition as the captured data can show areas needing refinement. Before we dive into the specific talent acquisition metrics, let's define what these metrics are.

Put simply, talent acquisition metrics are data points that measure the effectiveness of a talent acquisition team's effort. These metrics track the progress of various stages of the recruitment process and provide insights into how well the recruiting team is performing. Picture this as a roadmap that helps companies find where they are succeeding and where there is room for improvement.

Why do we track and collect Talent Acquisition metrics? The collection of data allows Talent Acquisition Leaders like me to measure and use these metrics to evaluate key recruitment processes and improve your recruitment strategy over time. By using them effectively and continuously monitoring the progress against established benchmarks or KPIs for talent acquisition, you can adjust your approach and optimize your recruitment efforts for greater success. In other words, a data-driven approach to Talent Acquisition helps show how effectively and efficiently the organization is hiring.

In this ever-evolving talent landscape, companies that embrace this data-driven approach using metrics are more likely to stay ahead of the competition and secure a steady stream of top-level talent. Deciding which metrics to track isn't easy as there are so many. Hundreds, in fact.[27] What to track should be figured out company-by-company, as each organization has unique needs and objectives. Through tracking metrics, you can optimize a data-driven hiring process and get tangible evidence of how successful your recruiting process is at your organization rather than relying on intuition.

Here are a few Talent Acquisition metrics that will give some insights so you can take your job search strategy to the next level.

COST PER HIRE

Cost per hire helps measure the total amount associated with recruiting to fill an open position. Measuring cost per hire provides a benchmark for driving recruitment costs down, allows you to keep an eye out for rising recruitment costs, and helps inform future recruitment budgets. It is measured by the total recruiting costs invested in finding and hiring candidates.

Cost per hire is calculated by dividing the internal and external recruitment costs by the total number of hires in a set period. Internal costs include your talent acquisition team's salaries, any employee referral bonuses, and the salary of the people conducting interviews. External costs include job advertising, immigration fees, recruitment agency fees, and recruitment software subscription costs.

TIME-TO-HIRE

Time to hire (or "time to fill") is the time it takes to hire a candidate for a position. Measuring hiring time usually begins at the application stage from when contact is first made. Time to hire is calculated by counting the days between the application and the moment a candidate accepts the position. Your time-to-hire averages should vary according to the requirements of every position.

A long hiring process can increase the cost per hire, and unfilled roles can lead to added expenses. While some positions can be filled in under 45 days, high-demand roles such as data engineers or key leadership roles can take over a few months.

OFFER ACCEPTANCE RATE

The offer acceptance rate measures the percentage of job offers accepted by candidates. A high offer acceptance rate suggests that the organization's recruitment process, compensation packages, and employer branding resonate well with candidates, leading to a more successful talent acquisition strategy.

A low rate may indicate a need to review and improve the recruitment process or other factors influencing candidate decision-making, such as work-life balance, career development opportunities, and company culture. By monitoring the offer acceptance rate, companies can identify areas for improvement and implement changes to enhance their attractiveness to prospective employees and secure top talent.

DIVERSITY HIRES

Diversity recruiting is one of the ways that companies can increase diversity and create a more inclusive workplace. Diversity metrics focus on the representation of underrepresented groups in the hiring process. Measuring diversity metrics such as gender, race, ethnicity, and other demographic factors can help TA Partners identify potential biases in their recruitment process and make informed decisions to improve diversity.

Regularly tracking diversity metrics can help TA Partners ensure a more inclusive hiring process and promote a diverse workforce. By tracking and analyzing diversity metrics, you can gain insights into your current state of Diversity & Inclusion efforts, identify areas of improvement, set goals and targets, and evaluate the impact of your actions and initiatives.

SOURCE OF HIRE

Source-of-hire is one of my favorite metrics. They show what percentage of your overall hires entered your pipeline from each recruiting channel or source. Tracking source-of-hire is more effective than tracking source of candidates because you want to know where the best performers are coming from. It can show whether your careers page generates quality candidates or whether your top candidates come from job boards, social media, referral programs, or external recruitment agencies. For example, a Talent Acquisition team may have the following targets as they manage their requisition load and overall hiring activities:

- Recruiter Sourced: 40%

- Employee Referral: 30%

- Applied: 20%

- Conversions 5%

- Agencies: 5%

The data above shows that most hires come from the recruiter's sourcing efforts to reach out to passive or nurtured candidates. Also, the organization has a healthy pipeline of employee referrals, and research shows that getting a referral is a cheaper and faster way to hire, generally produces a better hire, and lowers the turnover rate at your company.[28] Lastly, this reveals that only 20% of total hires come from those who applied through the career page.

As you can see, you can use the source-of-hire data to make decisions such as ramping up social media, investing in a premium ad on job boards, or switching recruitment agencies. Many Talent Acquisition Professionals want to know where the best hires in the organization have come from so that they can put more resources into these channels.

MICHELLE'S STORY

The Internship Advantage

Michelle is the University Relations Manager at a high-tech company, with over a decade of experience managing college programs. At her current company, they typically hire around 20 interns each summer, focusing on about 15 universities across the United States in what she calls "strategic relationships."

Michelle highlights the reasons her company invests in their internship program. "We hire college interns for several reasons," she explains.

"Firstly, interns bring a fresh perspective to our organization. They challenge the status quo and introduce new ideas to our teams."

A key advantage of internships is that companies are willing to train interns. "Interns are coachable talents who are more likely to adapt and learn the latest skills and tools from universities," she says. Furthermore, interns often become excellent full-time hires after graduation.

For Michelle's company, internships are a valuable way to gauge a student's potential by observing their performance in a real-world setting. "You get to see their skills and work ethic as an intern and might choose to convert them to full-time employees based on their performance," she admits.

Like Michelle and her team, many other companies have robust University Relations programs. They focus on hiring entry-level talent with potential - to find the right candidate who would ultimately be a good culture fit for the company. According to a survey, slightly more than 68% of employers offer their interns full-time jobs. Almost 82% of students accepted these offers. This data shows that 56% of college students are more likely to land a full-time, rewarding career after an internship.[29]

❦AN INSIDER'S VIEW ❦

You can measure university recruiting success in many ways, from the volume you can recruit to the strength of your relationships with universities to the performance of college grad new hires and far beyond. Here are a few key metrics that companies may track as a way to measure their college recruiting efforts and support a data-driven hiring process:

- 40% of engineering interns are from underrepresented backgrounds.

- 60% of GTM interns are from underrepresented backgrounds.

- 75% of interns are hired from targeted universities.

- 20% of interns are hired from sponsored organizations.

- 50% of interns at the senior level are converted to full-time hires.

Some organizations use internships to address gender diversity within their organization. For example, they may target specific organizations like the Society of Women Engineers (SWE) to increase the candidate pipeline and hire more women into technical roles. They may also sponsor events with organizations like Women in Revenue to connect and hire female members for sales, marketing or other revenue-generating roles.

There you have it - the ins and outs of a recruitment process. You now understand that data collection and metrics are essential for Talent Acquisition Leaders who strive to refine and enhance their recruitment processes for efficiency. There are certainly some general metrics that companies should care about, but the organization's hiring goals will be the deciding factor on what holds the most weight.

Keeping a close eye on crucial metrics allows TA Partners to gain valuable and discover unique insights into the effectiveness of their hiring process and identify areas needing improvement, ultimately resulting in better hires. At the same time, now you know how companies tend to measure the success of their recruitment efforts and leverage data into their decision-making process.

DATA-DRIVEN APPROACH TO JOB SEARCH

Using AI for job search activities is not wrong. It can be beneficial. For example, ChatGPT or Gemini can help improve your résumé or tailor your cover letter to a specific job posting. It may optimize your application to align with the required skills (or keywords) for a job opening. AI tools are emerging and can simplify the online application process for you, but that is not enough to secure a job. Having a data-driven mindset can be a powerful tool for you as well.

How can you apply a more data-driven approach to your job search process? Applying to online job opportunities alone and leaving it up to chance if someone gets back to you should not be your only strategy to secure an internship or entry-level job. As you may recall in **Figure 6.1**, automation processes are abundant, so connecting with an actual person will take more effort.

To avoid the black hole, **Figure 6.2** highlights a few examples of how to leverage data and insights to your advantage—instead of simply applying to jobs and hoping for a response.

Action	Data-Driven Mindset
Connect with your Career Center and learn who the repeated companies that attend their career fairs or other on-campus events	• Check if these companies consider your university as a targeted university. • If so, find out what all of the on-campus activities they plan to participate in. • Research types of interns they have hired in the past
	• Network and learn from their experience about the company; ask for informational interviews.

Research alums who worked previously as an intern or now work as full-time at your targeted company.	• Ask what they thought made their internship success that led to a full-time job. • Find out who their mentors were while working as an intern; connect with them on LinkedIn. • Gain further insight into their work environment; learn from their journey that helped them be successful. • Learn if they have a company-wide employee referral program
Research if your targeted companies have a University Relations Manager or College Relations Program Manager.	• Find out what their upcoming sponsored events are at your university. • Learn if your university is a targeted university for entry-level talent. • Who are the company representatives that come to your campus (e.g. HR, Alumni, Hiring Managers, etc.); ask for their advice about accessing jobs there
If you are an underrepresented student, find out what companies have diversity initiatives.	• Seek out affinity groups on campus and connect with alums that were past members. • Connect with University Relations Managers at your targeted companies and learn if

	diversity hires are a focused area or if they have any upcoming diversity events that you can register and attend. • Ask company representatives if they have employee resources groups (ERGs)
If you have an opportunity to interview for a role, ask the interviewer if the position is a "new role" or a "backfill" role.	• If new, find out the cause of the need for the role → new project, new investments, etc. • If a backup, ask if they converted the previous employee or if there are concerns about the manager, team or culture issues that lead to a departure.

Figure 6.2: Example of a Data-Driven Action Plan

Knowing these data-driven metrics is essential because you can incorporate them into your job search strategies to increase your focus, to boost efficiency and ultimately enhance the success of your search. By embracing a data-driven approach, you are turbocharging your job search process to track, measure, and improve your chances of landing a position and empowering yourself to understand the motivation from the other side - the employer.

🐂 Let's Be Bullish:

A data-driven mindset allows you to use data to track, measure, and improve your success. For example, you can track your overall job search progress and activities. The first step in applying a data-driven approach is to decide what quantifying variables you want to use, as shown in

Figure 6.3. Different metrics may be more suitable for other goals, industries, or preferences, but some common ones to consider are the number of applications you have sent, contacts at the company, date applied, responses received, interviews scheduled, follow-up emails, offers received, and time spent on job search activities.

Date Applied	Company	Position	Internal Contact?	Application Status	Follow up email	Standing Status	Time Spent
12/15/23	ServiceNow	Business Strategy Specialist Intern	No	Received			
12/26/23	Adobe	Finance Intern	Tracy M.	Initial Call	Thank you email sent	Waiting for update	1 hour
12/26/23	Dynatrace	Customer Success Intern	No	Received			
12/26/23	HP	Customer Service Intern	No	1st Round	Thank you email sent	Scheduling next round	2.5 hours
12/26/23	Teradata	Data Science & Analytics Intern	Susan T	2nd Round	Thank you email sent	Sent References	4 hours
12/26/23	Snowflake	Finance Analyst Intern	No	Initial Call	Thank you email sent	Gave availability	1 hour
12/26/23	Google	Business Analyst Internship	No	Received			
12/26/23	Apple	Database Management Intern	No	Received			
12/26/23	Tesla	Data Analyst Intern	Amy B	2nd Round	Thank you email sent	Waiting for update	3.5 hours

Figure 6.3: Example of Data-Driven Tracker

Data alone is only helpful if you take action, and care to analyze it to uncover valuable insights into our job search approach.

As shown in **Figure 6.3**, the number of applications sent can show how active you are in searching for opportunities. The number of responses received can indicate how effective your applications are in attracting employers and TA Partners. The number of interviews scheduled can demonstrate how well you match the requirements and expectations of the roles you apply for. The number of offers received can illustrate how successful you are in convincing employers that you are the best candidate for the job. Lastly, the time spent on job search activities can reveal how efficiently you manage your time and resources for your job search.

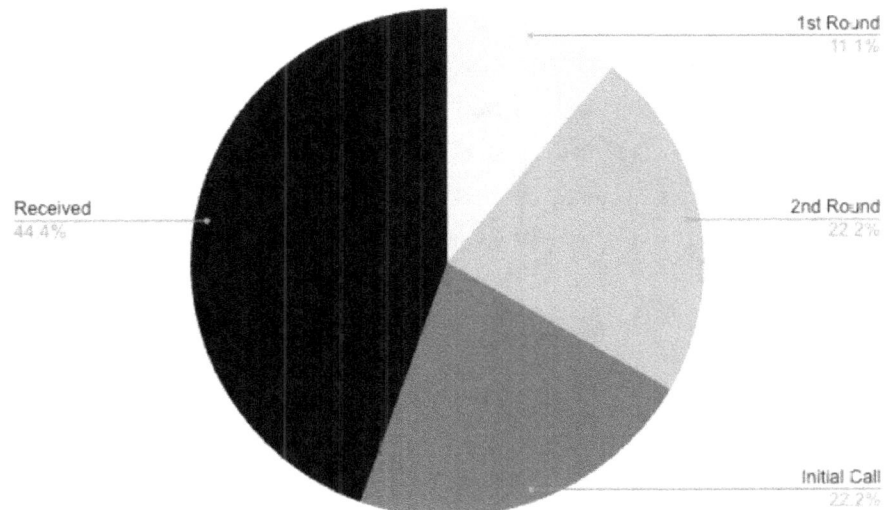

Figure 6.4: A Visual Dashboard of a Tracker

You, as the job seeker, can gain a competitive edge in your pursuit of job opportunities by strategically leveraging a data-driven mindset. Analyzing trends, application-to-interview conversion rates, and relevant industry-specific insights enables you to tailor your approach to meet job requirements. With this information, you can build your job search dashboard, as shown in **Figure 6.4**, to centralize your data and visualize your overall journey so you can spot trends and patterns. With data-backed insights, you can make targeted and meaningful connections that align with your career goals.

THE 3ʳᴰ DIMENSION – PARENTS IN THE MIX

Before we close out **Chapter 6**, let's talk about something most job search guides skip over—**your parents**. While you're juggling classes and applications, there's a third dimension in the mix that can add unexpected pressure: well-meaning family members who are eager (sometimes *too* eager) to help.

Whether your parents have been in the background or deeply involved in your college experience, the job search can stir up all kinds of emotions— for *them*. And that pressure has a way of leaking into your day-to-day grind. Their questions, suggestions, and comparisons might come from a place of love, but let's be honest… sometimes it's just a lot.

It might sound like:

- "Have you applied to that job your uncle told you about?"
- "Why haven't you heard back yet?"
- "Your cousin already has a job lined up…"

The intentions are usually good—but the pressure is real. And when you're already trying to manage your own timeline, interviews, and rejection emails, the last thing you need is a parent hovering over your shoulder, adding more noise to the process.

Here's the honest truth: **you can't control your parents' anxiety, but you can control how you involve them.**

HOW TO INVOLVE YOUR PARENTS WITHOUT LOSING YOUR MIND

1. Set Boundaries Early

Let them know what kind of support *is* helpful—proofreading a résumé? Practicing an interview? Great. But you'll be handling the applications, recruiter emails, and follow-ups yourself. Employers need to see *you* taking the lead.

2. Use Their Network—But Own the Follow-up

If your parents offer to introduce you to someone in their network, don't brush it off. That connection could be helpful—but make sure *you* are the one reaching out and driving the conversation. You're not asking for a job. You're asking for insight and building relationships on your own terms.

3. Express Your Independence, Gently

Explain that you're trying to build confidence by doing this yourself. Over-involvement from parents—even if well-meaning—can signal to employers that you're not ready to operate independently. That's not the impression you want to leave behind.

4. Get Backup If You Need It

Some conversations with parents can get tense. If things feel heavy, talk to a trusted mentor, advisor, or career counselor who can give you some perspective—and help you explain things to your family in a way that reduces friction.

BULLISH PRO TIP:

Build a simple "progress tracker" or job search doc you can choose to share with your parents. It gives them peace of mind and shows you're being thoughtful—without inviting daily commentary (refer to **Figure 6.3**).

And if you'd rather bring your parents into your process in a healthy, structured way, stay tuned for **Chapter 12**, where you'll learn how to use the **Bullish Career Canvas** to map out your plan and communicate it clearly—not just to yourself, but to anyone who wants to support your goals.

Now, let's recap.

Let's Recap!

- Talent acquisition metrics are a core part of data-driven recruitment.

- These metrics help companies assess the effectiveness of their hiring process—what's working, what's not, and where to focus.

- AI tools can help make your résumé more relevant and tailored, but they aren't a silver bullet. Securing a job still requires strategy, preparation, and follow-through.

- Companies rely on these insights to prioritize top channels and candidates—saving time, money, and energy.

- Use this insider knowledge to your advantage during your search, interviews, and performance reviews. Speak their language.

- Following these tips helps your application stand out, avoid the dreaded black hole, and move you one step closer to your next opportunity.

And remember: the more you understand how hiring works behind the scenes, the better positioned you'll be to beat the system—and be Bullish.

CHAPTER 6: THE BLACK HOLE, IS IT REAL?

Key Takeaways

NOTES:_____

_____

_____

_____

_____

_____

_____

ACTIONS:_____

_____

_____

_____

_____

_____

_____

Pause & Reflect

Before You Enter Part Three – You Ain't So Bad

By now, you've learned what separates the average candidate from the standout. You've explored the power of personal branding, internship performance, and career storytelling. You've also seen how perception, preparation, and networking can shift your entire trajectory.

Take a moment to reflect:

- What do people see when they look at your online profile or résumé?
- Have you turned classroom and internship experiences into compelling stories?
- Are you leveraging relationships—or just collecting them?

The next stretch is where confidence gets tested—and built. Let's find out what you're really made of.

PART THREE

"YOU AIN'T SO BAD"

- Rocky Balboa

7

CHAPTER

READY, SET, GO!

When's the right time to start preparing for your future? Spoiler alert: it's sooner than you think.

Whenever I'm invited to a university event—whether it's for networking or a guest speaker series—I always enjoy walking through campus and feeling the energy in the air. Students dart from one place to the next, juggling everything from lectures and assignments to social plans and exam prep. That constant motion reminds me of my own college years—filled with friendships, academic milestones, and memories I still cherish.

At these events, I get to connect with students from all backgrounds and majors. And no matter the setting, one question almost always comes up:

"When should I be looking for an internship?"

It's a great question—and an important one.

Internships are a powerful launching point. They give you an edge in the application process, help you build real-world experience, develop essential job skills, and clarify your career interests. But many students wait until later in college to pursue one, usually in the summer when their class schedules ease up or after they've declared a major. That's not a bad strategy—but it's not the only one either.

RUPALI'S STORY

Behind the Internship Curtain

Rupali is a University Recruiter focusing on emerging talent for a high-tech company. She has worked for about eight years with branded companies supporting their college relations efforts. "I love working with students, and that's why I've concentrated on this as an area of my focus," she says.

Rupali is one of three team members who oversee the recruitment of these internship roles and the overall management of her company's internship program. They work tirelessly to ensure the program's success with university officials, hiring managers, mentors, and interns. She explained that her team has a robust college relations program and shared the following details of her team's calendar of events, as shown in **Figure 7.1**.

Month	Deliverable/Action
September/October	Managers requesting summer interns must obtain budget approvals from their business leaders and finance. They must have clear learning objectives and identified projects that students will work on.

November	Upper management approves and communicates the headcount plan for the upcoming summer. Based on the total number of interns needed, our college relations team can begin to work on recruitment strategies.
December	This is when we commit to the Fall/Spring campus activities with our targeted universities. This includes posting the roles. We see a surge of candidates applying after the holidays.
January	We have a few schedules of college recruitment activities: • Informational Sessions (virtual/in-person). • Campus-wide/Major-specific Career Fairs. • Update company information on Handshake. • Finalize sponsorship details with diversity-focused partnerships/organizations/regional conferences.
February/March	This is a busy time of screening and interviewing. We start extending offers by early March, hoping to close candidates by the end of the month.
April	By mid-April, the majority of all our internship roles have been filled. We will begin the onboarding process for all selected Interns
May/June	Internship Program Kick-off. Program elements include:

	• CEO Welcome • Meet the Mentors • Interns Bootcamp/Company Overview • Dept Information Sessions/Workshops • Intern Team-Building Outings
July	• Internship Program comes to an end. • Final Project Presentations/ "Demo Day" • Mentor Evaluations/Interns Feedback
August/September	• Capture feedback and comments (mentors/students). • Reflect on recruitment strategies. • Debrief on interns' overall performance. • Determine if any rising seniors will be converted for early offers post-graduation.

Figure 7.1: Internship Program Calendar

Rupali shared, "At the end of each summer, with the students returning to their fall semester, we regroup and undergo a period of assessment that allows us to recalibrate and prepare for the coming year." She explained how they invest time in evaluating mentors, information sessions, and students to optimize their program for identifying potential hires. They also explore specific hurdles and challenges they face so they can make necessary adjustments to maintain a positive candidate experience for future intern hires.

Investing in early talent is a long-term commitment. Internship programs are seen as a strategic method for recruiting and nurturing talent, even in difficult economic circumstances. "We are aware of the financial restrictions and budget limitations we encounter each year with our college program. We maintain high standards when choosing our interns," Rupali stated. "We must demonstrate our value as we contribute to our overall Talent Acquisition strategy of being a key asset in attracting the upcoming generation of talent to our company.

Like Rupali's company, many organizations invest heavily in internship programs to identify and hire top early career talent each year. As shown in **Figure 7.1**, such a program may differ by business type and company size. However, you will find many similarities when you compare the objective of having such a program in place, which is identifying top talent from specific academic disciplines.

Is it ever too early to get started to search for an internship (or can you be too late)? There is always time to begin seeking professional experience, as discussed in Chapter 4. Companies continue to invest in internship programs, as we learned from Rupali's story, hoping to build their future leaders. If you plan to seek an internship, you should start looking 3-5 months before you would like to start, as you now see the calendar of events in **Figure 7.1**. Unlike traditional jobs, many internships hire candidates well before their start date.

College students should consider an internship after their sophomore or junior year. *Why after sophomore or junior year? Well, there are a few reasons:*

- Open opportunities: Most internships are only available to rising juniors or seniors. Traditionally, most companies have reserved internship slots for college juniors and seniors. The reasoning makes sense: upper-level students have locked in their majors, completed classes related to their chosen fields, and theoretically have more work experience. While there are different exceptions, most internships are open to these specific class years. Read the qualifications section of the job description.

- Early talent recruitment: Many companies use internships to source for entry-level positions. They want to attract interns who have experience behind them and students closer to graduation. This means employers try to hire interns to whom they eventually want to convert and extend full-time entry-level offers. For example, according to PwC's company's internship page, over 90% of their interns get full-time offers.

  If a company wants to hire immediately the following year, then upper-level students are the better choice, but sometimes, they play the long game and want someone they can coach, train, and mold into an excellent hire, so an enthusiastic and bright underclassman wins out over an apathetic upper-level student. Another possibility is that they just want a quick resource for a specific project and do not care about hiring; at this point the school year makes no difference. It is just your skills, personality, and experience that matter.

- Career readiness: While you do not need to be set on your career path or know what kind of job you want by your sophomore or junior year you are more likely to be decided on your major and have a better sense of what you are interested in versus when you just arrived at college.

The most important part to remember in your job search process is that when you are going to do the internship, it is often far from when you are applying. As I explained earlier, many companies open their internship applications early before the internship occurs.

AN INSIDER'S VIEW

When do you need to start your application if you want to land an internship during your sophomore or junior year? **Figure 7.2** illustrates a guide to assist you through four stages of the career readiness process, starting with your first year at college.

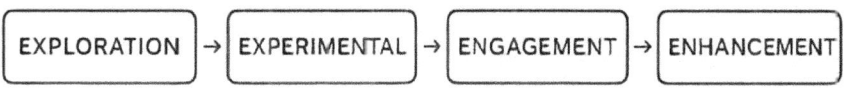

Figure 7.2: Four Stages of Career Readiness

FRESHMAN YEAR

Welcome to college! Use this time to adjust to your new college life and explore subjects you might be interested in. Connect with upper-level students and ask them about their internship experiences. This is a valuable way to get insights about opportunities, companies, or industries that might not be on your radar — as well as inside application tips on how to get started.

With so many new experiences, it is easy to overlook career-related activities. But with no deadlines looming, the first year of college is the perfect time to seek information on various fields.

EXPLORATION STAGE:

☐ Become familiar with campus offices and services.

- Meet other students and make new friends.
- Seek academic support.
- Make study commitments.

☐ Meet with a Career Counselor.

- Major/Minor Exploration

- Discover the importance of self-awareness and identify how your personality, skills and interests align with possible career options.
- Ask for help with obtaining job shadowing experience.
- Activate your Handshake - set up profile and explore the platform.

☐ Create a first draft résumé (translate your high school experience to college).

- Visit your career center for résumé tips and tools.
- Create a résumé and seek feedback from a career counselor.
- Research the dos and don'ts of résumés.

☐ Get Involved!

- Join a student activity/organization of interest.
- Research volunteer work on and off campus.
- Participate in residence hall activities.
- Begin to develop communication, collaboration, and teamwork skills.

☐ Attend Career Fairs.

- Begin to create your professional network.
- Connect with company representatives.
- Learn about occupations and employers in your field of interest.

☐ Network Opportunities.

- Meet with advisors, professors and older students to learn more about major(s) of interest and different career paths.

- Focus on data gathering of companies, market sectors, industries, and any other information.

SOPHOMORE YEAR

As you enter the spring semester of your sophomore year, you are starting to blast through your general education requirements and move into more degree-specific coursework. This is such an exciting time as you begin learning more about topics you are passionate about. Sophomore year is an ideal time to press into some degree-specific involvement. That may be a club, picking up research in a lab, joining a student association on campus, applying for work-study, or applying for their first summer internship.

EXPERIMENTAL STAGE:

☐ Meet with a career counselor:

- Leverage career exploration tools if you are still unsure of your major and possible career path.
- Connect with a peer advisor and share your career development plan for the year.
- Create your professional social media presence using LinkedIn.
- Develop a comprehensive search strategy for finding work experience.

☐ Get Involved!

- Join a major-related student organization and actively develop your leadership skills.
- Research opportunities through service learning and volunteering.
- Interact with guest speakers and college personnel to build connections.

□ Connect with alums:

- Attend Alumni networking events to meet professionals in your field of interest.

- Seek a mentorship relationship by others who have been where you are.

- • Request a job shadowing experience.

□ Engage with employers:

- Attend career fairs and other career events.

- Observe others networking, practice elevator pitch.

- Learn about opportunities now that you will be able to apply for later.

- Discover what type of roles they have a history of hiring from your university.

□ Networking Opportunities:

- Begin networking with employers through career panels, job fairs, and industry mixer events.

- Conduct at least two Informational Interviews with professionals.

- Meet with professors to pursue undergraduate research or service-learning opportunities.

- Ask family, friends, professors, and career counselors about internship or part-time job leads.

JUNIOR YEAR

The job search process continues! This time, update your résumé with your previous internship experience. Include any new skills, classes, projects, extracurricular activities, or work experience you have done in the past year. This means your résumé will need a refresh! You will also likely have some new experiences to draw from for your internship interview answers.

ENGAGEMENT STAGE:

☐ Meet with a Career Counselor:

- Discuss your career development plan for the year.
- Update your résumé, Handshake profile, and LinkedIn for employers to see.
- Conduct research to determine the types of entry-level roles for which you might qualify.
- Participate in job search-related workshops such as mock interviews, résumé and cover letters, networking, and any other activities that will prepare you in your job search.

☐ Stay Involved!

- Take leadership / executive roles in student organizations, volunteer opportunities, and extracurricular activities.
- Be able to articulate leadership skills in interviews, on professional documents, and through interviewing.

☐ Networking Opportunities:

- Develop strong relationships with your professors.
- Expand your professional network.
- Begin to market yourself - know your strengths and promote what you have gained.
- • Reach out to alums and professionals on LinkedIn to conduct informational interviews.

- • Fine-tune your interview with professionals and seek their feedback.
- • Join local chapters of national organizations related to your chosen field or career path.

☐ Job Search Activities:

- Continue to update your résumé and LinkedIn profile.
- Narrow down prospective companies for employment.
- Research and apply for internships, research opportunities, or part-time job opportunities.
- Read professional journals in career areas of interest.

SENIOR YEAR

You are almost there! Research internships are available for recent graduates if you still need to do an internship or want more internship experience before transitioning to a full-time entry-level position.

Graduation and a degree may be right around the corner, but there is much to do during this final year of college. TA Partners start interviewing and making offers as early as the Fall for full-time positions that begin in May or June. Seniors who put off their job search until the last couple of months of the spring semester or the summer after graduation will have missed many opportunities.

ENHANCEMENT STAGE:

☐ Meet with a Career Counselor:

- Reflect and create an action plan for your career path.
- Update your résumé and have it critiqued by a career counselor.
- Start applying for jobs as early as the Fall timeframe.

- Polish communication style to convey an effective elevator pitch with confidence.
- Attend job search and other related workshops, including on-campus interview.
- Participate in a practice interview to sharpen your skills.

☐ Stay Involved!

- Continue to pursue leadership positions in student organizations.
- Mentor peers looking to develop their competencies and skills.
- Act as a resource to lower-level students; consider becoming a tutor.

☐ Networking Opportunities:

- Use LinkedIn to identify alums and conduct informational interviews to expand your network.
- Attend career and networking events (on and off-campus), company presentations, and more.
- Use your network to identify opportunities.
- Connect with mentors and colleagues via LinkedIn from your previous internship or part-time roles.

☐ Job Search Activities:

- Shift job search into high gear.
- Update and finalize your LinkedIn profile.
- Exhibit your class projects electronically or in a digital portfolio.
- Request recommendations via LinkedIn from advisors, mentors, and professors.

- Tailor your résumé and cover letter to each position for which you apply.
- Actively monitor postings in Handshake and other job sites
- Track the status of each position and follow-up on applications.
- Clean up your social media accounts.

You should take specific steps to help you explore various career options. Just like a final exam, your internship job search or program selection is not something you should 'cram' for at the last minute. It takes time, reflection, and different experiences to help you define your career goals.

Remember, deciding on a career is a process, and it will not happen two weeks before graduation. Start exploring as early as your first year because it is never too early to start thinking about your career goals. **Figure 7.2** provides a year-by-year guide to keep you on track for career readiness. With the four stages of the career readiness process, I am confident you will be much more prepared to find a career that suits your passions, values, interests, and goals.

🐂 Let's Be Bullish:

Visit your university's career center's website to see if they have career readiness planning tools available for you to use. If not, you can use a simple worksheet like in **Figure 7.3** to help you develop career-related skills and experiences during each year of your college life. This worksheet allows you to identify activities to help your journey toward career readiness. You can fill out this worksheet on your own and discuss your plan with your career counselor.

Year	Planning Activities	Notes
Freshman	• • •	
Sophomore	• • •	
Junior	• • •	
Senior	• • •	

Figure 7.3: Four-Year Career Readiness Worksheet

With this approach, you can progress through the worksheet in order or pick and choose the activities that will help you make confident decisions about the career paths you would like to pursue. Another way of looking at this worksheet is to use the backward planning concept, where you start planning from the end and work backward from there (see **Figure 3.2**). If you are thinking backward with career goals, imagine yourself getting hired for your dream role.

What sets you apart? What steps did it take to get into the role? With this in mind, you can create a reverse timeline on paper with captured activities that maximize your chances of success. Remember, as always, that you are not alone in this work. If you break your job search process into baby steps, you will realize that finding an internship or your first job ain't so bad after all. Career counselors or peer advisors care about your future and are available to support you.

Let's Recap!

- Internships are often decided months in advance—get on the radar early.

- Understand the four stages of career readiness: Exploration → Experimental → Engagement → Enhancement.

- Each stage builds on the last—don't skip ahead before you've laid the foundation.

- Strategic actions (like networking or targeted applications) can leapfrog you ahead.

- You've got more potential than you realize—now's the time to channel it.

CHAPTER 7: READY, SET, GO!

Key Takeaways

NOTES:_____

_____

_____

_____

_____

_____

_____

ACTIONS:_____

_____

_____

_____

_____

_____

8

CHAPTER

_____

THE DECODER RING

This sucks! That's what you often hear from job seekers when they feel that a company has ghosted them after they had a series of interviews.

"Why aren't they calling me?!!!"

Even after you've sent a thoughtful thank-you email to the hiring manager, the silence is deafening.

"How should I read into this lack of communication or silence? Do they still want me?"

Whether you're a college student or a seasoned professional, many job seekers express the same anxiety and confusion—wishing they had a **decoder ring** to help unravel the mysteries of a company's hiring process.

You know the drill: you search for job opportunities, apply, and eventually land an interview. You feel good about how it went—you connected with

125

the interviewer, answered their questions well, maybe even made them laugh. You don't know exactly what happens next, but you're hopeful. You think you nailed it.

And then... you wait.

You wait.

You wait some more.

Until you just want to scream.

Maybe you do scream—in your car, your room, or into your pillow. Or maybe you jump on TikTok to rant about how ridiculous it is that a company ghosted you after three interviews and all that effort. Or you just sit there, spiraling, imagining everything you *wish* you could say to that company you once thought was perfect for you.

But before jumping to conclusions or assuming a company has intentionally designed a frustrating waiting game to torture you—take a breath.

Let me explain the hiring process to you.

ANNETTE'S STORY

Decoding The Waiting Game

Annette is an experienced corporate recruiter for a management consulting firms based in Chicago. She shared that her company primarily hires from top universities, including undergraduates and MBA students, and that it generally takes between 60 - 90 days from posting a job to filling the role with a qualified candidate. "We like to think we set a high bar when hiring talent, and we will take as long as needed to find the candidate we feel best fits the team and the firm.

The last thing you want to do is rush and take shortcuts with any offers, as you may regret your decision later," she explains.

Annette is responsible for filling an average of 20-25 requisitions per quarter for her firm. For each role she works on, she screens over 50 candidates, sometimes more, and she presents only a few candidates to the hiring manager to determine who to pursue. "My job is to source and narrow down the list of qualified applicants who I believe have the right skills and would be a culture fit for us," she says. Once the hiring manager and the interview team have interviewed enough candidates, the challenge is to gather everyone's assessment. "Most times, trying to get their feedback feels like herding cats. It may take a few Slack nudges, email reminders, or even chasing down folks to complete the candidate evaluation forms, but I eventually get them all," she adds.

Annette, her hiring manager, and others who interviewed the candidates will then meet for a debrief meeting. "We discuss what we learned during the interviews and how we assess each candidate against the role and, at times, against one another," she continues. A few outcomes may result from these debrief sessions. They are the following:

The team may want to bring back a candidate for another round of interviews to delve deeper into a particular area discussed during the debrief session.

If a candidate moves towards the offer stage, then the hiring manager may request to check references or seek backchannel references from mutual acquaintances or colleagues. The team may not be satisfied with the current batch of candidates and may want to see more profiles before making a final decision.

Annette may need to start the search process with new candidates at any point in the above scenario. "That's why it takes 60-90 days to make a hire at our firm," she explains. Does that mean that silence always means they are working through the process? "Yes, until we reach a point where we have extended an offer to a finalist and officially received an acceptance.

Our process may be lengthy, and our decision timeline does not always pair up well with candidates who need to know their status," she says. "Once a candidate interviews with us, they want to know instantly where they stand. With our high volume of applicants, I can't accelerate our decision-making process to appease everyone. We will take as long as it takes," she concludes.

As a job seeker, waiting for a hiring decision can be nerve-wracking. Have you ever wondered why it takes employers so long to make a hiring decision? As highlighted in Annette's story, multiple factors contribute to the long process.

Although the hiring process may vary by industry, company size, and position level, companies like Annette's firm typically follow some variation. Some companies may require multiple rounds of interviews, panel interviews, presentations, skills assessments, or reference checks before deciding. This can take time as various stakeholders within the company need to approve each step in the process.

Additionally, some companies may have strict hiring policies that require all candidates who applied to be vetted thoroughly before they can extend an offer. While these internal processes can be frustrating for job seekers, they are implemented to ensure that the company hires the best-fit candidate for the role.

INTERVIEW DEBRIEF SESSIONS

An interview debrief session is a meeting with the hiring team – hiring manager, recruiter, and other interviewers and stakeholders – to discuss each candidate that has been interviewed and make informed decisions together. This gives each stakeholder a chance to share their thoughts while they are fresh to come together and deliberate on candidates, minimizing the chances that anything is forgotten.

Over the last twenty years or so, hiring has become an essential part of company success.[30] It used to be a more cyclical, rote process that focused on "putting butts in seats," but now many companies have come to realize that it is vital for their revenue to get hiring right the first time around. It is not just about hiring people to do the job – it is about hiring the right people, in the right job, with the right skills, to do the job.

Especially for fast-moving companies and interviewers with busy schedules, immediately writing down post-interview notes and observations is not necessarily easy or appealing. This is common in early-stage startup environments, which need more formal processes and workflows. These environments tend to be scrappy and lean, quite informal, and decision-making is generally collaborative and fast.

On the surface, the purpose of the debrief session is simple: make a decision on the candidate. For selection teams who decide to have debrief sessions after an interview has concluded, a little bit of time investment after every interview can go a long way towards making critical hiring decisions. It calibrates the hiring team on what good looks like, what is essential, and what is nice to have in a candidate. It is also a time to understand the candidate's previous work and personal culture orientation to ensure that it aligns with the organization.

Interview debrief sessions directly answer issues with cyclical hiring, miscommunication amongst the hiring team, and quality of hire. It allows each team member to voice their opinions about the candidates they are considering. It does not matter how long the debrief is or whether it is synchronous or asynchronous. It is successful if the team dedicates the time needed for the debrief. Such a review process reduces the likelihood of bad hires, which may lead to a waste of time, lost money, cultural impact, or the painful process of letting someone go.

AN INSIDER'S VIEW

There was once a time when a simple statement from the hiring manager such as "I like the candidate, let's hire" or a hand gesture of a "thumbs-up" or "thumbs-down" signal decided the fate of a candidate. Times are different now, and as you've learned, much more is involved when deciding whether or not a candidate is good fit for the role.

These debrief sessions, as highlighted in Annette's story, are structured discussions when evaluating candidates. The following are insights into what happens behind closed doors:

1. BEFORE THE DEBRIEF SESSIONS.

   All participants have recorded notes, scores, or ratings for every candidate they interviewed before the debrief sessions. These are captured via email or applicant tracking systems (ATS). Each team member is asked to review their highlights of their interview with the candidates, including evidence gained from the candidates' conduct during the interview, and from the way in which answers were communicated.

2. THE FACILITATOR.

   The recruiter or hiring manager who oversaw the interview process typically leads and moderates the conversation, and other colleagues should defer to their leadership. The recruiter is responsible for keeping track of time and making sure all teammates are heard equally. This is important so that no one team member monopolizes the conversations and ensures that everyone has an opportunity to share their perspective.

This is no easy task. I have been in many debrief sessions where these candidate discussions have been very heated, and loud voices have chimed in at the same time. By the end of the debate, team members must feel they have been heard with respect.

3.   THE DISCUSSION FLOW.

Step 1: Introduce the discussion. The facilitator starts by explaining the purpose of the debrief, providing an overview of the process, and sharing how many candidates will be discussed. He/she establishes necessary ground rules, such as not interrupting another colleague's speaking time and respecting each other's opinions.

Step 2: Review the candidates. The selection team will adhere to a specific sequence while evaluating every candidate. Each team member involved in an interview will have the chance to provide their ratings and feedback on the criteria essential to the position, referred to as the "rubric." A criterion on a rubric is a specific trait or skill that you would like the new employee to possess (see **Figure 8.1**).

These sessions allow the team to explore why there are differences of opinion and invite commentary to compare them. Here are specific questions typically asked in these sessions to engage in conversation:

- What did you like most about this candidate?

- Did this candidate possess the core competencies we are seeking for the role?

- Can this candidate make an immediate impact, or will they require training?

- How well matched are this candidate's interests with the job and our company culture?

- Are there any concerns you have with this candidate that would prevent them from moving forward?

- Does this candidate align with our company values?

- Has this candidate demonstrated evidence of key leadership competencies?

Step 3: Review the candidate pool together. Once all candidates have been discussed, the selection team usually examines their scores in aggregate, as seen in **Figure 8.1**. These sessions allow additional time to discuss candidates who performed similarly, and for team members to offer any last-minute commentary about candidates that were not captured when candidate evaluations were completed.

Step 4: Make a decision. This does not necessarily have to be a final decision on who to hire for the position. Still, at the end of the debrief session, a hiring manager should be able to walk away with actionable next steps for the candidates discussed.

To support this structured decision-making process, many organizations use scorecards like the one shown below. Each interviewer rates the candidate based on a defined rubric and provides their input on role alignment, competencies, and projected impact. The average score offers a quick snapshot, while the detailed breakdown helps highlight patterns, disagreements, and strengths or weaknesses across the panel.

Key Areas	Criteria	Interview Questions	Andy	Sue	Liz	Bob	Average
Role	Job Alignment	What are your career goals? What are your goals in the next 3 years and how do they fit into your career aspirations?	3	3	4	3	3.25
Competencies	Ownership	Tell me about a time when you took on a responsibility that was not technically part of your job description.	2	2	3	2	2.25
	Adaptability	Think about a time when something you worked on did not go to plan. What is your approach to those situations?	3	3	4	3	3.25
	Multitasking	What is your approach to prioritization and time management? What have you done that has worked in the past vs. has not worked as well?	4	3	4	3	3.25
	Humility	Tell me about a time when you disagreed with a decision made by your team or manager. How did you approach the situation?	4	3	4	4	3.75
Key Outcomes	Within 3 months	What would you like to achieve with the first few months of hire?	3	2	3	2	2.5
	Within 12 months	What would you like to achieve with the first year of hire?	3	3	3	3	3
Work Sample	Mock Sales Presentation		3	3	4	2	3

Figure 8.1: Example of a Candidate Evaluation Scorecard

It's important to know that when a selection team member is interviewing you, there is usually a focused area such as a "rubric" to which this interviewer has been assigned. If you can gauge this before an interview, it will help you prepare for the questions that may be asked. If not, look

133

at the job description and identify the required competencies mentioned in the job posting. Interview rubrics are a powerful tool that aims to help employers better evaluate job-related competencies where the traditional unstructured interview process often falls short.

While interview rubrics can vary from company to company, they should ideally include the following four key components to give you an even playing field. Rubrics serve as a hiring equalizer—they reduce bias, bring structure to subjective conversations, and ensure that every candidate is assessed using the same criteria.

Here's what most rubrics include:

1. **Competencies necessary for the role.** An interview rubric should outline the specific knowledge, skills, and behaviors required for success. These competencies may include areas such as teamwork, decision-making, customer service, or adaptability.

2. **Structured interview questions.** Each competency is paired with a targeted interview question, giving you a clear opportunity to demonstrate your capabilities. If you don't have direct experience, be prepared for hypothetical questions that assess how you would respond in relevant situations.

3. **Rating scale for performance.** Rubrics typically use descriptive performance labels—such as *Proficient*, *Developing*, and *Underdeveloped*—to guide scoring. Rubrics help standardize evaluations across interviewers.

4. **Evidence-based notes for justification.** Finally, rubrics include a section for interviewers to record specific examples or observations from the conversation. This evidence helps justify each score and provides a shared understanding of what different performance levels look like.

Competencies	− −	−	+	+ +	Notes
Communication Explanations and thoughts were precise, organized, and logical.					
Culture Fit They are a good add to our company culture.					
Experience / Qualifications Necessary skills or qualifications through past work experiences.					
Customer Focus Consider customers' point of view when making decisions.					
Problem Solving Solves problems using data, logic, and insight.					
Adaptability Is flexible and open-minded when dealing with others.					

Figure 8.2: Generic Interview Rubric

If you find yourself in an interview with a rubric (see **Figure 8.2**), the structured approach can give you a clear roadmap to showcase your skills and abilities most relevant to the job.

Here are some tips to help you make the most of the opportunity and stand out as a top candidate:

1. **Understand What Might Be On The Rubric In Advance**. Before the interview, research the company and carefully review the job posting to identify key competencies. If former candidates have shared their interview experiences online (such as on Glassdoor), check for clues about what might be evaluated. Pay attention to repeated themes and terminology—those words often mirror the rubric itself.

2. **Listen Carefully To The Interviewer's Questions.** During the interview, actively listen for keywords or behavioral cues that align with the job description. If a question isn't clear, don't be afraid to ask for clarification. Doing so shows thoughtfulness and your commitment to fully understanding the role.

3. **Use The S.T.A.R. Method.** Rubric-based interviews often rely on behavioral questions to assess competencies. Organize your responses using the S.T.A.R. method—**Situation, Task, Action, and Result**—to deliver concise, compelling answers. (If you're unfamiliar with this method, meet with your Career Center Counselor for guidance.)

4. **Provide Concrete Examples**. Whenever possible, back up your responses with concrete examples from past experiences, class projects, or leadership positions. These examples should align with the competencies in the job description. Quantify your

achievements and highlight any specific accomplishments that demonstrate your abilities

5. **Be Honest and Authentic.** While it's important to tailor your responses to the rubric, don't over-engineer them. Interviewers value sincerity and want to get a true sense of who you are. Authenticity can be a powerful differentiator, especially when multiple candidates have similar qualifications.

6. **Follow Up Thoughtfully.** After the interview, send a thank-you email to the interviewer to express your appreciation for the opportunity to interview. Use this chance to reiterate your interest in the role, explain how your skills align with the competencies you were asked about, or expand on how you can add value to the team based on what you uncovered in the interview session. Think of it as a final way of pitching yourself one more time for the role.

SKILLS VS. COMPETENCIES

You may be asking yourself, *What the hell is a competency?* When reading a job description, there is often a list of the core competencies captured as requirements for someone to succeed in the role. Many may recognize this as "skills". It might seem as if these two words are interchangeable – but it's not quite right to describe "competency" as a synonym of "skill".[31]

There is a genuine difference between these two terms. If you are looking for a new job or are keen to understand how to advance in your career, you must recognize the differences. Realizing the difference will help you:

• Review job descriptions more effectively to more accurately understand which skills and competencies the company is looking for and why.

- Add skills and competencies to your résumé in a way that resonates with the reader.

- In a job interview, explain your skills and competencies and directly relate them to the job you are applying for.

- Understand any skills gaps and which competencies you may need to build on to advance your career, both now and in the future.

HOW DO SKILLS AND COMPETENCIES DIFFER?

What are skills? Skills are the specific learned abilities needed to perform a given job well. Examples range from handling major accounts to coding software applications, depending on the particular role. There is a distinction between hard skills and soft skills – a hard skill is a technical and quantifiable skill that a candidate may demonstrate through their specific qualifications and professional experiences, and a soft skill is a non-technical skill less rooted in particular jobs. An example of a hard skill could be computer programming or proficiency in a foreign language, whereas a soft skill may be time management or verbal communication.

Therefore, a skills-based job description might prefer you have a BA in accounting or finance, at least two years of accounting experience, and strong proficiency in Tableau, QuickBooks, or Excel.

What are competencies? Competencies are the knowledge and behaviors that lead a person to be successful in a job. Examples of competencies include the improvement of business processes, strategic planning, and data-based decisions. Competencies explain how an individual's behaviors bring about the desired results. As with skills, there are various types of competencies – including core competencies, which any successful employee requires to be promoted through an organization.

So, skills usually focus on one's ability to perform a specific role or function and can be learned through education and training. At the same time, competencies are types of behavioral traits and methods of thinking gained through experience, observation, and practice and are transferable between most roles.

Therefore, a competency-based job description also includes the need for analytical thinking, teamwork, and a client focus. Such job descriptions emphasize the candidate's qualities, the required skills, and the tasks they'll take on.

ROBYNN'S STORY

Competencies Drive Success

Robynn is a Talent and Learning Consultant who has collaborated with numerous business leaders on talent management initiatives, focusing on identifying essential competencies for their organizations. "Each company is unique, and I've helped them explore each competency, its relevance, and levels of mastery, from basic to expert," she says. "It is crucial that once we do this for internal employees, we also apply it to the hiring process to evaluate new hires."

Robynn explains that competency-based hiring is a recruitment strategy centered on assessing a candidate's skills, knowledge, and attitudes to determine the right fit for an organization.

Robynn has worked with many companies and has trained hiring managers to believe that competency-based hiring can be an effective tool for attracting top talent. It provides a framework for evaluation, allowing interviewers to focus on concrete behaviors and specific evidence to help with the selection process. "Focusing on the specific skills and knowledge required for a position, you can be sure that the candidates have the right experience from day one," she adds.

Competencies are the personal traits that can enhance performance in a specific role, leading to excellence rather than mediocrity.[32] These include soft skills and personality traits such as communication, enthusiasm, teamwork, decision-making, and resilience, all of which are difficult to identify or measure. "By honing in on specific competencies for the role, you gain a more accurate understanding of a candidate's potential for success in the organization," she concludes.

WHY DOES THIS MATTER?

Robynn explained the importance of competency-based interviewing. It helps hiring teams to see beyond the candidates who just talk or look the part, and it provides a specific set of answers, which can form the basis of a profile to measure candidates against each other. Asking candidates to share past examples of where they have demonstrated a particular competency, such as teamwork or resilience, strongly predicts their future behavior in similar situations. It is far more factual than asking candidates hypothetical questions about what they might do if faced with a possible scenario.

As a candidate, this allows you to demonstrate your skills in a detailed and specific manner. You may be asked to share an example of how you used or demonstrated that specific competency in the past. You can confidently tell your unique story and be able to highlight particular examples based on your college experience. If you have an interviewer asking questions that target a specific skill or competency, it will help you better understand what is expected from the role.

CLUES TO COMPETENCIES ON RÉSUMÉS

As a job seeker, you need to be aware that TA Partners, hiring managers, and interviewers of the selection team will not only review your résumé but also preview your LinkedIn profile or other social media platforms for clues to specific competencies or skills. For example, each competency or skill on the list below is followed by indicators of that competency that can be found on a résumé.

☐ Intellectual Curiosity

- Founded a successful business or organization.

- Worked on the business end of a student activity (e.g. newspaper, theater, fraternity, sorority, etc.)

- Held an internship requiring significant customer interface. (Success in the position and learnings from it should be probed in the interview.) • Worked on a research project.

- Has tried new things through learning experiences.

- Had a broad array of experiences (e.g. travel abroad, different types of jobs, varied extracurricular pursuits, etc.).

☐ Create Innovative Strategies

- Level of difficulty of college major.

- High grade point average/ class standing.

- Awards for academic, athletic, or other excellence.

- Participated in a class project that changed the way something was done.

- Part of a hackathon team focused on solving a problem.

☐ Inspire Commitment

- Led a group of peers over an extended period (e.g. several times had been elected captain of a team, president of an organization, etc.)

- Expressed passion, drive, and energy toward an accomplishment.

☐ Leadership Capabilities

- Coached a team.

- Led a group of peers through a successful venture (e.g. several times had been captain of a winning team, president of an organization or project leading to specific achievements, etc.)

☐ Champion Other People's Growth

- Tutored other students.

- Volunteered as a peer counselor or with a community group in a support role.

- Was a Resident Advisor in a dormitory.

- Spent a semester in another country.

- Participated in a particular program unrelated to college major.

☐ Drive For Results

- High grade point average/class standing.

- Awards for academic, athletic or other achievement.

- Recognition from a community group for service.

- Held a leadership role in a club or organization.

INTERVIEW QUESTIONS

The following section is divided into six parts, one for each competency mentioned above. Each basic question is followed by one or more additional questions to help you grasp how these probing questions contribute to providing as comprehensive a view as possible of one's abilities for a role. Hiring managers and interviewers tend to ask open-ended questions about particular behaviors or situations. (e.g. Tell me about a time when you exceeded a goal you set for yourself.)

These questions are the type that interviewers may be asked of you to provide evidence of your knowledge, skills, or experience for the job. The possible answers provided will help you gauge what would be weak or strong indicators. These answers are only examples, as candidates' responses may differ, but it is helpful to see how you should respond to such open-ended questions. Ultimately, it is up to the interviewer to exercise judgment in deciding if the answer received is strong, weak, or somewhere in between.

Intellectual Curiosity - shows a deep curiosity and good understanding of the global business environment.

• Breadth of perspective	• Customer focus and service orientation
• Business acumen	• Market understanding (including competitors)
• Spotting and creating opportunities	• Brand awareness

Interview Question	Weak Answer	Strong Answer
In the jobs that you have held, tell me about a time when you had to deal with a difficult customer. (What was it about the customer that was difficult? What	No experience with difficult customer or described ineffective response to customer.	Important customer presented a real challenge; able to turn the situation around; need analysis went beyond just data collection, reflecting deep understanding

did you do? What was the result?)		and resulting in the creation of fresh outside-in based ideas
Describe a situation in which you had to meet the varied needs of a number of people. (What was the situation? How did you learn about their needs? What did you do?)	No relevant experience; not able to learn needs of everyone	Understood needs of different people; devised effective solutions to satisfy everyone
From what you have learned about our Company, what do you think are the most significant factors affecting our business? (If a candidate doesn't mention market factors, ask: What market factors are significant?)	Naïve view of market; little knowledge of the Company; struggled to explain the Company's position in the market.	Had researched the Company, e.g., seen Web page, analysts' reports, etc.; had insight into complex market issues.
Can you describe a time when you capitalized on an opportunity? (What was the situation? What did you do? What was the outcome?)	Did not describe capitalizing on an opportunity or opportunity was obvious and of little benefit	Seized an opportunity that was not obvious to others; realized a substantial benefit from opportunity; describes an opportunity developed through deep understanding of the market and brought

		in reflecting 'outside-in' thinking.
Looking back on your college years, is there any opportunity that presented itself that you did not take? (What was it? What did you learn?)	No recognition (or admittance) of missed opportunities; did not learn from experience	Articulated important lessons learned; now evidences of increased focus on opportunities

Create Innovative Strategies - Develops and embeds simple, effective strategies that make us winners in the market. Encourages and disciplined risk-taking, while balancing short-term and long-term priorities.

• Strategic thinking and vision	• Risk-taking and decisiveness
• Analytical and cognitive ability	• Entrepreneurial perspective
• Project management and business planning	• Innovation and creativity

Interview Question	Weak Answer	Strong Answer
To what extent have you been involved in setting direction for a group or organization to which you belonged? (What was your role? Tell me about the	Little or no experience dealing with strategy; focused on short-term or tactical issues in groups	Played a pivotal role in helping a group deal with strategic issues; articulated a clear vision or purpose for the group

issues with which you had to deal.)		
Have you ever had to make a business case for one of your ideas? (How did you go about doing so?)	No experience preparing business case; no interest or enthusiasm for making business case	Described at least one well thought-out case, especially if not part of coursework
Assume that your family has a great recipe for chocolate chip cookies. It is so good people at school who've tested it have suggested you go into competition with Mrs. Fields and Famous Amos. How would you go about deciding whether or not to go into business? (What do you think you would need to do in order to launch your business?)	No idea of steps required; haphazard approach	Discussed systematic processes, including competitive analysis, cost revenue projection, etc.
Tell me about the most complex decision you've had to make under time pressure. (What did you base the decision on? About	Failed to describe complex decisions; procrastinated	Complex decision; well, thought out and timely

how long did it take to make it?)		
Have you ever questioned something you thought was wrong or unfair? (What did you do?)	Accepts status quo; no evidence of confronting; concerned with being liked or pleasing others	Has challenged the status quo; successfully confronted others

Inspires Commitment - Create a winning mindset by mobilizing people around vision, strategy and goals. Builds an understanding of its relevance. Develops an inclusive and high-energy environment. Earns trust by acting as a role model.

• Trustworthiness and integrity	• Persuasiveness and influence
• Personal impact and inspiration	• Listening and communicating
• Interpersonal skills	• Valuing differences and cross-cultural awareness

Interview Question	Weak Answer	Strong Answer
Give me an example of a time when you had difficulty getting along with someone. (How did you handle the situation? What was the result?)	Unresolved or relied on others to solve difficulties; avoided person; blames other people	Took responsibility for creating positive relationship; worked through difficult situation without external intervention

Describe a situation in which you personally have been responsible for motivating others. (How did you go about it? What was the result?)	No example, or insignificant goal, or goal people already motivated to achieve	Motivated others to achieve significant goal they wouldn't have reached on own; used techniques, e.g. team rewards, to generate enthusiasm
Describe a time when you had to change your behavior or working style to meet changing needs in your environment. How did you do that? Why was change necessary? What did you learn? What was the outcome?	No example, or insignificant change; unable to describe how they went about changing, what was learned or why change was necessary; negative outcomes without clear learning	Demonstrated appropriate adaptive behavior, clear understanding of need for change, willingness to leave comfort zone and try different behavior; able to articulate learnings
Can you tell me about a time when you found it challenging to relate to a person from a different background? (What happened? What did you do? What was the result?)	No example or did not try to improve relationship; avoided contact	Significant differences; took responsibility for relationship
Tell me about a time when your listening skills really paid off	No example, or minor benefit	Described positive benefit from listening

Tell me about a time when your ability to communicate was an important factor in achieving your goal. (What was the situation? What did you do? What was the outcome?)	No example, or communication had minor impact on achievement	Clear link between goal attainment and communication effort

Leverage Capabilities - Work across internal and external boundaries to maximize value through simple solutions.

• Teamwork and collaboration	• Organizational awareness
• Networking	• Company knowledge
• Cross-boundary cooperation	• Building partnership

Interview Question	Weak Answer	Strong Answer
Give me an example of a time when you were a member of a team that had difficult team dynamics. (How did you handle the situation? What was the result?)	Unresolved or relied on others to solve difficulties; avoided conflict; did not feel responsible for improving dynamics	Took responsibility for creating positive team atmosphere; worked through conflicts engaging team members positively

Describe a situation in which you personally have been responsible for mobilizing a diverse group of people over whom you had no direct authority to achieve a significant goal. (How did you go about it? What was the result?)	No example, or insignificant goal, or team already striving to achieve goal	Built on diverse strengths of others to achieve significant goal none would have reached on their own; aware of skill sets needed, identified people with those skill sets, and generated enthusiasm across those individuals to work together towards common goal
Describe the most valuable team experience you've had. (What was your role on the team? What did you learn that you could apply to a team in the workplace?)	Unenthusiastic about team experience; minor role in team success; no transferable learnings	Positive team experience; significant contributor to team's success; learned how teams operate effectively and able to articulate transferability
Have you ever been a team leader or captain? (If the answer was yes: What did you do to help the team work well together? What was the result?)	Little or no team leadership experience; did not actively attempt team building	Substantial experience as team leader; evidence of team success; actively promoted team process (e.g., used team building exercise)
Give me an example of a time when knowing	No credible example	Used knowledge of informal culture to

"how things get done" – at your school or on a job – helped you. (What made you decide you needed help? How did you figure out how to get it?)		achieve goal; cultivated a network
Describe a team you have worked on. (Who was on the team? What was your role? What did you like about the team experience? What didn't you like?)	Little experience with teams; preference for working independently	Many team experiences; sought out team projects; preference for working collaboratively with others

Champion Other People's Growth - commit personally to the performance and development of others, while considering the organization's long-term needs. Acknowledge and act on your own learning needs.

• Curiosity and eagerness to learn	• Coaching and mentoring
• Self-awareness and response to feedback	• Individual and team development
• Continuous self-development	• Career counseling

Interview Question	Weak Answer	Strong Answer

Tell me about a time when you actively sought out feedback from someone else in order to improve yourself. (What did you do after you received it?)	Never sought feedback, or sought feedback and didn't act on it	Sought feedback even when uncomfortable; improved based on feedback
Describe a time when you gave a person feedback. (How did you go about it? What was the outcome?)	Never gave candid feedback, or gave feedback but softened it, no indication of acceptance	Provided candid feedback in a difficult situation, person accepted it
What have you done during your college years outside of the classroom to expand your skills? (Describe how this paid off for you?)	No significant examples of skill building outside of the classroom	Took courses outside major; involved in campus or community activities; learned new skills and applied them
Describe a time when you volunteered for something. (What was it? What was your reason for volunteering? What were you expecting to learn? What did you learn?)	Did not seek out volunteer opportunities; did not build new skills	Actively volunteered; gained meaningful new skill

Tell me about a time when you were a role model or mentor for someone else. (Who was the person? What did you do?)	Never been role model, or mentor or expressed discomfort in role; did not leverage opportunity	Aware of influence; consciously set positive example

Drive For Results - Take accountability for delivering results. Continuously drive for operational excellence and simplicity in everything we do. Instill a sense of urgency.

• Drive and resilience	• Quality of contribution
• Goal and achievement orientation	• Initiative and confidence to act
• Follow through and reliability	• Stress tolerance and stamina

Interview Question	Weak Answer	Strong Answer
Tell me about a time when you had to work at a fast-paced environment (What kind of work was it? What did you do to maintain the pace? What was the result?)	Failed to describe an example of really working hard	Was driven by the opportunity to succeed; put forth extraordinary effort, e.g. worked every weekend for three months to finish project

Describe a situation where you overcame significant obstacles to get what you wanted. (What was the problem? What did you do? What happened?)	Abandoned or compromised goals because of obstacles	Succeeded despite significant obstacles
What do you consider your most significant work or school-related failure? (Why? What happened? What did you learn?)	Thrown off balance by failure; not tested (no examples of setbacks)	Worked harder and smarter after failure; articulated important lessons learned
Describe your most significant achievement. (What did you do? Why is it important?)	Modest achievement; not difficult	Specific and exceptional achievement; not ordinarily accomplished; pattern of setting and achieving meaningful goals
How have you kept track of progress on the project for which you were responsible? (Give me an example.)	Relied on limited information or inappropriate indicators to track progress; no evidence of periodic monitoring	Used available technology to track project; tracked multiple indicators; did his/her best to ensure that project was on time
Describe a situation where you saw a	Failed to describe a situation in which	Seized opportunity to solve problem

problem and took action to correct it. (What was the problem? What actions did you take? What was the result?)	he/she acted without direction	
Describe a time when you expressed an opinion with which others disagreed. (What was the situation? What did you do? What happened?)	No example or disagreement was insignificant	Has expressed an opinion with which important people disagreed strongly

🐃 Let's Be Bullish:

Much has been shared to help demystify the hiring process by giving insights into what is happening behind the scenes. For a quick exercise, look at a posted job description you are interested in. Could you identify the difference between skills and competencies? If so, then review your résumé and see if it needs updating to mirror the skills and competencies mentioned in the job description with those listed on your résumé.

If you are scheduled for an interview, would you be prepared to differentiate possible weak or strong responses that you may be asked during the interview? If not, schedule time with your career counselor for a mock interview and practice. To help tailor your mock interview session, I recommend that you share the job description or any other relevant application materials. Through practice, you build confidence and comfort for your upcoming interviews.

Let's Recap!

- The post-interview waiting period can feel agonizing—but don't waste energy stressing over things outside your control.

- Every company operates differently, and timelines vary. Delays don't always mean bad news.

- Hiring decisions often take 60–90 days from job posting to offer. Be patient and stay engaged.

- Behind the scenes, recruiters are navigating multiple layers of review, feedback, and approvals.

- You can't control the process—but you *can* improve your odds by mastering competency-based interviews and following up professionally.

CHAPTER 8: THE DECODER RING

Key Takeaways

NOTES:_____

_____

_____

_____

_____

_____

_____

ACTIONS:_____

_____

_____

_____

_____

_____

_____

9

CHAPTER

AM I READY FOR LINKEDIN?

There is a lot of confusion about LinkedIn. Some see it as a social media platform—like Facebook, Instagram, or TikTok. Others treat it like a job board. And in some ways, both views are correct. But unlike other social apps, LinkedIn is built for professionals. And unlike traditional job boards, it offers far more than just job listings.

To understand LinkedIn's value, it helps to zoom out.

The rise of the internet completely changed how college students search for jobs. In the past, you'd print out résumés, attend in-person job fairs, and hustle to make face-to-face connections. Today, it's much more common to apply online through platforms like Handshake, CareerBuilder, or Indeed.

The problem? Many students don't realize how inefficient that system can be.

Roughly 50% of online applications are never seen by a human.

Applicant tracking systems filter out candidates automatically based on keywords and criteria in the job description. With 118 to 250 applicants per posting, some recruiters only respond to 20–30% of candidates.[33]

That's why networking matters more than ever—and LinkedIn is where that networking happens.

According to Talent Acquisition experts, there's no substitute for direct human connection when it comes to job searching. About 80% of professionals say networking is essential to career success. In 2023, 70% of people hired had a LinkedIn connection at the company.[34] And applicants who received an employee referral were nine times more likely to be hired.

So, if you're only using job boards and ignoring LinkedIn, you're leaving opportunities on the table. It's time to stop treating LinkedIn like an optional tool—and start treating it like your professional launchpad.

According to a study, when looking for a job, most college students mainly focus on the employer's website (70%), followed by speaking with someone working for the company they wish to apply at (65%), getting information at their school's career fair (61%), various online job listing sites (58%), and the smallest number recognized social networking sites including LinkedIn (26%).[35] The statistics show that professional networks are not an important part in college students' job search. They do not use the opportunities to brand and market themselves to potential employers or TA Partners online.

About 95% of TA Partners from various industries use LinkedIn when searching for potential employees.[36] The widely recognized professional networking platform has approximately 1.1 billion members in over 200 countries worldwide, with over 40 million jobs posted.[37] Approximately 46 million LinkedIn users are college students or new graduates.

What does this all mean? LinkedIn is an invaluable resource for college students. Its mission is simple: help career professionals succeed through networking opportunities, job listings, news, and insights from other professionals.[38] However, I often hear from college students that they do not have significant work experience to showcase on LinkedIn, which might make students feel less confident, or they are being overlooked in a network filled with professionals who display years of experience compared to them.

NOAH'S STORY

Your LinkedIn Billboard

Noah is a Talent Sourcing Partner with experience in executive search and recruitment for several Fortune 500 companies. "As a seasoned Talent Sourcer, I always look for talent or leads, regardless of my current opportunities. I use various sourcing tools to build and curate pools of qualified candidates for my recruiters," he says. "Often, I feel like a detective, seeking that special unicorn with the right skills and best match for the team," he boasts.

Noah's primary focus is search, but it's a numbers game that requires proactive efforts. "Sourcing candidates takes time, patience, and persistence," he explains. "My main source for building a talent pipeline is LinkedIn. Like many other recruiters, I spend most of my time on this platform hunting for talent, viewing profiles, and contacting potential prospects primarily through LinkedIn InMail."

"When sourcing for internships or entry-level roles, I notice missed opportunities with college students," Noah notes. "It can be difficult for students to know where to start. Many of you are active on all social media channels except LinkedIn because it's not as fun; there are no friends to connect or chat with. You may feel that the content is not for you since everyone talks about jobs, articles, and content you wouldn't normally consume."

"LinkedIn is essential for college students. Your profile acts like your own personal billboard. Like all billboards on the side of the highways, the content must be engaging, tell a story, and show value. The earlier you begin, the more advantages you create for yourself and the better your chances of finding a job," Noah says. "LinkedIn is a platform that will evolve with you over time, depending on your professional needs, whether for job seeking, internship opportunities, or building your network with college alums or others."

WHY LINKEDIN MATTERS IN THE HIRING JOURNEY – THE BIG PICTURE

Before a company ever hires you, they're already thinking long-term—how you'll perform, grow, get rewarded, and eventually move on. This big-picture view is called the **Employee Life Cycle** (see **Figure 0.2**)

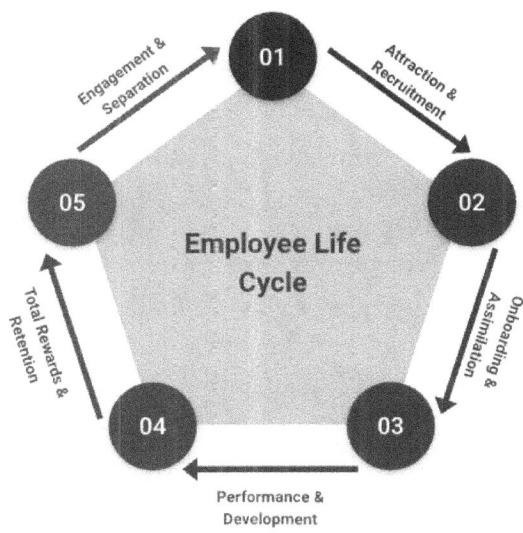

Figure 0.2: Typical Employee Lifecycle (Revisited)

Companies don't just fill roles. They build talent pipelines. And every step of your professional journey—from the moment you apply to the moment you eventually exit—can be mapped to one of these five stages:

1. **Attraction & Recruitment** – How you show up in search results, your résumé, and your LinkedIn profile all play a role in how recruiters first "notice" you.

2. **Onboarding & Assimilation** – What happens after you're hired and how quickly you adjust to your new role.

3. **Performance & Development** – How you grow your skills, earn feedback, and build your professional reputation.

4. **Total Rewards & Retention** – Your compensation, benefits, and the reasons a company hopes you'll stay.

5. **Engagement & Separation** – What happens when you're fully engaged… or considering moving on.

For now, your focus should be on **Stage 1: Attraction & Recruitment** —especially crafting a strong online presence through your LinkedIn profile. How you position yourself today can determine whether you're discovered tomorrow.

The rest of the life cycle becomes more relevant once you're in the workforce—but it all starts here, with your first impression.

WHY LINKEDIN MATTERS TO RECRUITERS

LinkedIn is not just a place to show off your digital résumé—it's one of the primary tools recruiters use to find talent. When a recruiter begins their search, they often don't start with a job board or a stack of résumés. They start with LinkedIn.

Why? Because LinkedIn has over 1.1 billion profiles, giving recruiters immediate access to a massive pool of potential candidates. Job boards might have a few hundred million users at best, but LinkedIn is where the talent pipeline lives and breathes.

Here are a few insights from a few Talent Acquisition professionals.

> *"When I go searching for people, I usually will search LinkedIn to find them. After all, there are 1.1 billion profiles, vs. what, a few hundred million at best on a job board."*
> — Talent Acquisition Leader

For recruiters—especially those focused on sourcing—your LinkedIn profile is often more important than your résumé. It's the first thing they see. And it's what drives outreach.

> *"If a résumé isn't provided yet, a person's LinkedIn profile will be the primary conversation driver. Again, this depends on the recruiter—but since I primarily source talent, I lean more on a LinkedIn profile than a résumé."*
> — Senior TA Partner

Most recruiters don't post every job publicly. Some are paid specifically to find candidates quietly. That means your profile needs to speak for you—even when you're not actively applying.

> *"My clients do not post their roles. They pay me to find prospects to interview. And guess where my team hunts…drum roll please… LINKEDIN! Make a headhunter want to DM you."*
> — Senior Agency Recruiter

But here's the catch: if your profile isn't complete or doesn't include the right keywords, it may never show up in a recruiter's search—no matter how qualified you are.

> *"If I come across your profile and can't see much detail about what you've done, I'll be forced to skip over it."*
>
> — Senior Sourcer

And for those of you just getting started? Don't worry. Recruiters aren't expecting years of experience—they're looking for initiative and potential.

> *"I don't expect students to have long job histories on LinkedIn. I'm just looking for signs of initiative—clubs, projects, internships, even volunteer work. Anything that tells me who you are and what you're interested in."*
>
> — Campus Recruiter, SaaS Company

> *"LinkedIn is your digital handshake. If you're not on there, I can't introduce you to hiring managers—even if you're the perfect fit."*
>
> — Executive Recruiter, Finance Sector

If you're not on LinkedIn—or your profile is missing key skills, experiences, or keywords—you're essentially invisible to a large portion of the hiring world. A recruiter can't reach out to you if they can't find you. So, let's fix that.

So, when is the right time to create a LinkedIn account?

If you've made it this far in the chapter, the answer is: *right now.* No more waiting until you have a "real" job title or a long list of experiences. Your profile is your first handshake with the professional world—and it matters.

It's not just about being online. It's about being discoverable.

Your résumé shows what you've done. Your LinkedIn profile shows where you're going. And if you're already on the platform, it's time to step up your game and create a profile you're proud of—one that showcases your value, your story, and your potential. One that TA Partners can't ignore.

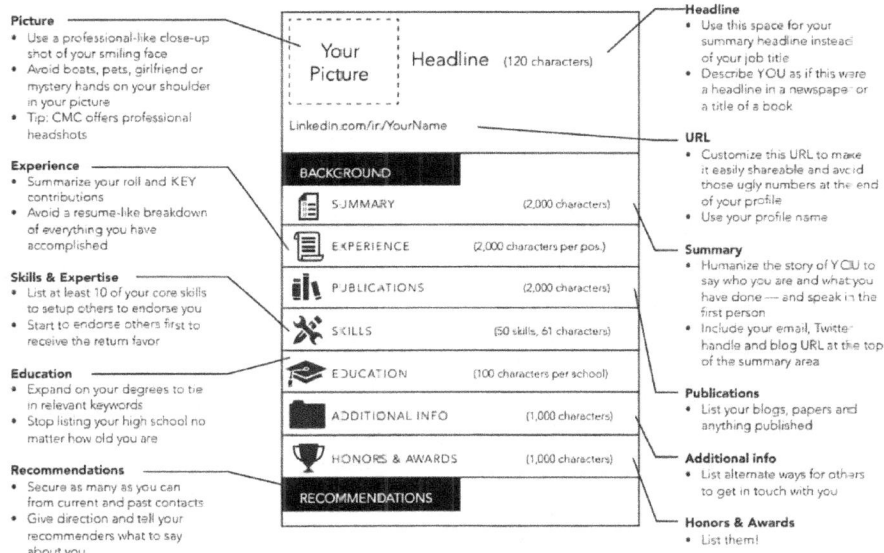

Figure 9.1: The Anatomy of a LinkedIn Profile

So, what are the keys to a great profile? There are many but here are ten of my favorite tips to quickly improve the appeal and effectiveness of your LinkedIn profile (see **Figure 9.1**):

1. **Have a great headshot.** Be yourself but make it professional. Consider the background behind your head - keep it simple. Be aware of your facial expression, not being overly enthusiastic or overly serious. It is essential to add a picture that represents you the way you want to be perceived.

165

2. **Insert a background picture behind your headshot** to tell more of a story about yourself. Click the pencil icon that allows you to edit your profile. From there click the pencil icon that sits in the wide image space. Many people have the default filler image from LinkedIn or a meaningless image of a mountain or an ocean - that says nothing about you professionally. Personalizing your background image with something that represents your professional passion. For example, if you want to pursue a career in education, choose a banner photo of you at the front of a classroom.

   You can pull an image off Google or check out Unsplash, Pixabay, or Pexels sites for free, high-quality images. Canva is a great app to create the background image within the LinkedIn template or use your university's LinkedIn banner as an option. Be sure to view your profile on both a desktop and mobile, so that you choose an image that works well for both.

3. **Use a strong headline**. Your headline appears below your name in your profile. You are more than just your current job title, which is what many of your profiles currently show as your headline. What you write greatly affects how you show up in search results. Instead of saying, for example, 'Events Coordinator,' you could say, 'Marketing Events Coordinator. Consumer-Focused, Brand-Builder, Digital Marketing Expert.

   Please note that you only have 220 spaces for your headline, which LinkedIn increased from 120 spaces, but I would say somewhere between 100-150 characters is perfect.

4. **Write an impactful 'About' section.** This is the first section below your headline. Many students fail to write anything in that

section because they find it intimidating to write about themselves. I highly recommend that you do not make this same mistake, because this is a significant missed opportunity to share your story and incorporate relevant keywords. This section can give you a strong overview of your skills and experience (years, industries, functional areas) and what you're looking for. Here's an example for a job seeker: "Former Division 1 collegiate athlete with four years of experience in marketing and ticket sales. Have expertise in project management, marketing planning, and social media buying in the sports and entertainment industries."

I would love for you to add keywords in your 'About' section too, check the next tip for that.

5. **Leverage keywords.** Put a keyword paragraph highlighting your areas of expertise at the end of your 'About' section. This is a great way to align yourself with the positions you are interested in and come up higher in recruiter search results. Explain who you are, what you currently do, and any experience or projects you are particularly proud of. If you are in your final year, you could include final class projects to highlight your research skills and interests.

You can add up to 50 skills to your profile. However, I recommend that you try to focus on up to fifteen that define who you are and what you are good at. Try to include ones that are particularly important to the career path that you are interested in. If you are unsure which skills employers are looking for, look at recent job postings or other LinkedIn profiles of professionals that work at a targeted employer.

6. **Put the actual details of your work experience.** Remember that TA Partners know that you are a college student. Please do not write a LinkedIn profile that makes it sound like you have been working in business for ten years. Many profiles just list past positions with no details on what they were responsible for and the impact they had. Instead, think about everything that you have done during college. You may also wish to include positions of responsibility that you had for extracurricular activities, such as being a Teacher's Assistant or club member. Also, be consistent with your formatting across jobs – bullets or a short paragraph, not both.

7. **Include visual examples.** There are many places in your profile where you can add examples, such as images, videos, or files to showcase your work. This includes class projects, presentations, or reports that can be featured here too. Build a list of technical skills you learned, such as industry knowledge or working with any specific software. For the soft skills you developed, organize a list of examples of how you demonstrated them, as this will become handy in future behavioral-based interviews.

   This is a great way, especially in your work experience section, to bring your expertise to life in more than just words. LinkedIn provides a unique opportunity in this section to enhance your standard résumé by allowing you to tell a more comprehensive story.

8. **Continue to update your LinkedIn profile.** If you recently completed an internship, it is time to make that experience shine on your LinkedIn profile and your résumé. The benefit of any internship is that it significantly strengthens your "Work Experience" section. Although the experience was an internship,

the opportunity acts like a full-time job. It will undoubtedly be mentioned again during your following job interview. Showcasing that you have work-related experience, an elementary understanding of a particular industry, and the relevant foundational skills will give you a leg-up in attracting interest from a future employer.

9. **Have a recommendation written about you.** Ideally have two to three recommendations about you and at least one from the current year. This section shows up at the bottom of your profile and is an easy way for people to read your profile to get a better feel for your professional reputation. Recommendations are essentially mini versions of the letters from professors, Teacher Assistants, mentors, coaches, or former managers would provide you. This is a great way to acknowledge your skills and abilities.

Because recommendations are more detailed and require thought, I suggest taking the time to think about who would want to write your recommendation and asking them. Preferably, anyone you have had a positive relationship within the past would make for a great LinkedIn reference.

Note: I do not advise jumping into LinkedIn's automated 'Request a recommendation' feature. Proper etiquette is to reach out to your contacts first to ask them if they are willing to do this for you. Otherwise, it can come across as pushy if they just get your request through LinkedIn.

10. **One last thing.** As with any résumé, first impressions are important, so ask a trusted mentor, advisor, or Career Center Counselor to check and review your LinkedIn profile for errors. Believe me, there are many found on people's profiles, even

seasoned professionals. The bottom line is that if you are on LinkedIn, bring your A-game. Investing a bit of time in making the updates above helps set a solid foundation to maximize the platform's potential and move your career forward.

Most people, even college students, agree that networking and connections can help you increase your chances of finding jobs, business opportunities, sales leads, and customers. Have you ever heard the old saying, "It's not just what you know; it's who you know." 85% of jobs get filled through networking.[39] Networking is a critical part of your job search success.

At its core, LinkedIn is all about people. If used correctly, it is a social media tool that helps you establish a professional online presence personal brand, advance your career, and build your professional network.

AN INSIDER'S VIEW

Congratulations, you have built the perfect LinkedIn profile, now what?

TA Partners turn to LinkedIn because it offers a wealth of information about candidates, including their work history, education, schools, skills, recommendations, and professional network. LinkedIn profiles serve as comprehensive résumés, giving TA Partners a snapshot of a candidate's qualifications and experience. As a job seeker, having a solid presence on LinkedIn can significantly enhance your chances of being noticed by TA Partners and landing an internship or your first job.

So let me share with you how TA Partners conduct their search for candidates on LinkedIn. TA Partners employ various strategies to find candidates on LinkedIn, depending on their specific requirements.

Here are some common methods they use:

LEVERAGING LINKEDIN RECRUITER

LinkedIn offers a premium service called "LinkedIn Recruiter," which provides TA Partners with search capabilities and additional features to streamline their candidate sourcing process. This is a paid subscription that many companies pay for so that their recruiters can utilize to source, attract, and hire great candidates (see **Figure 9.2**).

With LinkedIn Recruiter, TA partners—both in-house and within professional services firms—can tap into a broader talent pool and gain deeper insights into candidate profiles.

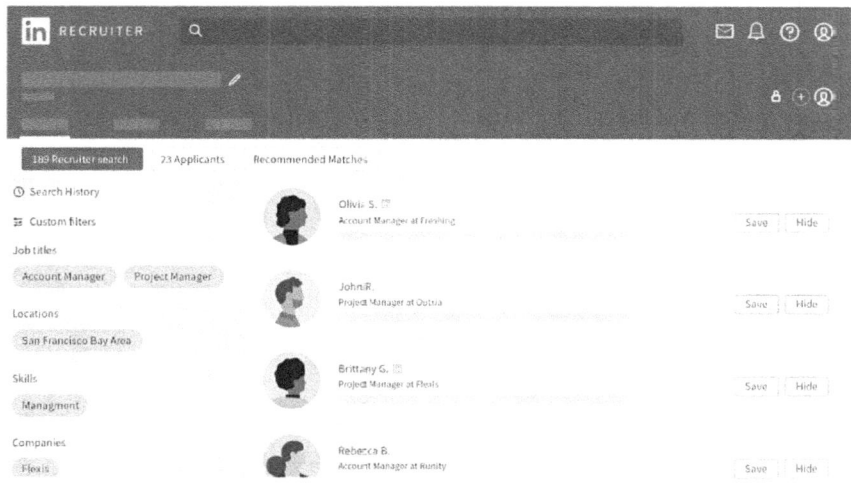

Figure 9.2: LinkedIn Recruiter

LinkedIn Recruiter allows TA Partners to save searches, track candidates, and send personalized messages directly through the platform. It enables searching for candidates using various criteria, including job title, location, industry, and skills. This tool allows TA Partners to efficiently manage their candidate pipeline and stay organized throughout the hiring process.

USING KEYWORDS AND FILTERS

Once TA Partners understand the role details, they often start their search by entering specific keywords related to the job they are trying to fill. These keywords can include job titles, skills, industry keywords, and location. LinkedIn's search algorithm then generates a list of profiles that match the search criteria, with the most relevant matches appearing at the top.

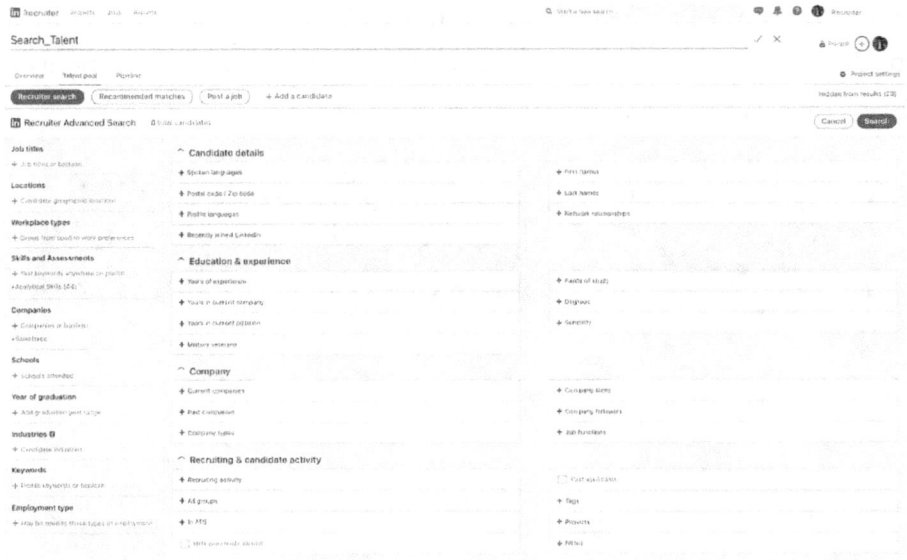

Figure 9.3: LinkedIn Recruiter Advanced Search Filters

TA Partners can further refine their search using advanced search filters, such as years of experience, education level, and company size (see **Figure 9.3**). These filters help TA Partners find candidates who meet their specific requirements.

When TA Partners views a candidate's LinkedIn profile, they look for specific information and indicators demonstrating the candidate's qualifications and potential fit for the role.

Here are key elements that TA Partners pay attention to:

1. **Complete and Accurate Information** – TA Partners expect to see a well-rounded profile that includes comprehensive information about a candidate's work history, education, and skills. Incomplete or inaccurate information can raise red flags and deter TA Partners from pursuing a candidate further. It is important to ensure that all sections of your LinkedIn profile are completed with accurate and up-to-date information.

2. **Relevant Work Experience and** Skills – TA Partners focus on a candidate's work experience to assess their suitability for a role. They look for relevant positions, class projects, responsibilities, and significant achievements that align with the job requirements. Additionally, TA Partners understand that candidates who are college students or graduates may not have extensive experience, so they pay attention to the skills section of a profile and look for key competencies that match the desired qualifications for the position.

3. **Professional Headline and Summary** – A candidate's professional headline and summary provide TA Partners with a quick overview of their expertise and career goals. TA Partners appreciate concise, compelling headlines that capture a candidate's professional identity and value proposition. The summary section should provide a more detailed narrative of a candidate's experience, skills, and career aspirations.

4. Recommendations and Endorsements – LinkedIn allows users to request recommendations from colleagues, professors, mentors, advisors, and managers, providing valuable social proof of their skills and accomplishments. TA Partners view recommendations as evidence of a candidate's credibility and professional

relationships. Similarly, endorsements from connections can reinforce a candidate's expertise in specific areas.

The more relevant content you can provide on your LinkedIn profile, the better chance you will have to stand out from the crowd and differentiate yourself from other candidates.

🐂 Let's Be Bullish:

Is your LinkedIn profile ready for prime time? A well-crafted LinkedIn profile can be the key to landing an internship or your first job. Take a moment to sign up for LinkedIn and start creating your profile. Invest time to ensure your profile picture, headline, summary, experience, education, and certifications are current and showcase your unique professional brand. Engage with your network and stay active on the platform to increase visibility and build relationships with potential employers.

If you need additional assistance setting up or refreshing your LinkedIn profile, visit your career center for support and great tips!

Let's Recap!

- The wonderful experience about college is you will constantly be building your network.

- While you may view LinkedIn as a tool for working professionals to network and find new jobs, it is also a tool for college students that will help you stand out to TA Partners and hiring managers.

- LinkedIn can be just as important as your résumé. In fact, you can think of LinkedIn as an online résumé!

- LinkedIn can be used to join groups, write articles, and post photos and videos that highlight your professional journey.

- A well-optimized LinkedIn profile not only helps boost your visibility to be noticed by TA Partners but makes it easier to connect with past colleagues and peers to grow your professional network.

CHAPTER 9: AM I READY FOR LINKEDIN?

Key Takeaways

NOTES:_____

_____

_____

_____

_____

_____

_____

ACTIONS:_____

_____

_____

_____

_____

_____

_____

Pause & Reflect

Before You Enter Part Four – Why So Serious

Things are getting real. This isn't about getting in the door—it's about showing up with clarity, intention, and confidence. You've now tackled real interviews—from prep to follow-up—and learned how to spot red flags, pivot when needed, and take ownership of your story. You're not just exploring—you're applying pressure in the right places.

Take a moment to reflect:

- Do you understand how success is measured where you want to work?

- Have you practiced articulating your value—clearly and confidently?

- Are you still just applying… or are you positioning yourself as the ideal candidate?

The final chapters are about turning preparation into momentum. Let's finish strong.

PART FOUR

"WHY SO SERIOUS?"

- The Joker

10

CHAPTER

QUEST? I'M ALREADY ON A QUEST

One thing that I often encounter when working with college students on their job search activities is a sense of fear and anxiety. As they get closer to graduation, they feel a sense of panic about finding a job, which can be stressful. I totally understand how exciting and relieving it is to see the end of your college career. It is also easy to feel overwhelmed when the structure guiding your day-to-day halts suddenly post-graduation. You no longer have an academic advisor or professors lining up your semester schedule of classes and spelling out the steps for success.

In addition to the uncertainty of the job search and the looming number of applications, résumés, and interviews, it is not unusual to feel lost when looking for your next big opportunity. The job search process can knock your self-confidence and have you doubting your future goals more than ever.

One of my students I worked with by the name of Sharon, sent me the following text message after a couple of engagement sessions:

"What are some steps I could take next year to ensure that I'm at least somewhat prepared to apply for jobs when I graduate? I started networking like crazy. Many of my friends are interviewing, and I'm not getting calls like they do. What am I doing wrong? I'm scared that it's already too late for me to do well once I'm out of here."

My response to Sharon was simple, *"Don't freak out. Take a deep breath...you'll be fine."*

Think of the job search process as your personal "quest" that takes practice and refinement. While being proactive means applying for jobs and putting yourself to the test in interviews, it also means continuing to learn new things. Take it from me, someone who has interviewed thousands of candidates and has also experienced my fair share of interviews. It is a great way to continue discovering things about yourself and to reaffirm what you do and do not want professionally. If you have this mindset, the job search process can be a bit lighter, more fun, and less serious.

Do not feel weary, like in the case of Sharon. Job hunting can be exhausting. Instead of measuring yourself against your friends or others at school, focus on the facts in front of you - *What made you successful in getting into the university? What are your strengths? What have you learned from your time at the Career Center? What skills do you possess, and how do you use them to your advantage? Do you know you are about to earn a college degree due to your hard work?*

Having the truth about your skills and capabilities in front of you will help negate any unhelpful self-talk that may derail you from preparing yourself to enter the workforce because it is hard to deny the truth. You got this!

So, while ultimately overthinking when you are looking for an internship or your first job is not unusual, it can still be risky, both for your morale and confidence. So, take advantage of this free time to stay sharp! Continue to learn new things, adjust your profile, refine your storytelling skills, talk to people, and apply for jobs. Taking action is still the best way to boost your morale, so no more hesitating or overthinking - take things one day at a time.

EMILIO'S STORY
Persistence Pays Off

Emilio has worked as an in-house recruiter in the media industry for over ten years. "I'm not going to lie, it's tough work, but it's lots of fun, and it can be gratifying," he explains. "I have a chance to talk to candidates daily and share what makes the company, the team, and the job unique. If there's a match, I know I helped the company find the best candidate for the job."

"When it comes to students or new college graduates, it is a bit challenging as I am hiring more for potential versus experience," Emilio states. A soon-to-be graduate contacted him from a local university where the company did not actively recruit. He expressed a strong interest in a marketing position and asked to meet. "We did not have any openings at the time, so I told him to send his résumé, and we would keep him in mind if anything suitable came up," he continues.

"The college student called me every two weeks and developed a good rapport with me," he shares. He was professional and articulate about his skills and his desire to work for us. I decided to bring him in for an informational interview. When we met, I was quite impressed, especially with his class projects and portfolio—he had done his homework on the company," Emilio says.

Emilio decided to call a couple of marketing managers and ask if they would give him a courtesy interview. They agreed and were so impressed that they decided to hire him!

As I mentioned in **Chapter 6**, applying only to online jobs and praying for responses cannot be your only strategy to find an internship or land your first job, but many do it. Just go on TikTok or Instagram, and you will hear many rants from other job seekers getting ghosted or never hearing back from employers.

If you are entering the job market, hunting for a job can feel intimidating as job seekers are pitted against one another to snatch up the latest job openings. Fortunately, it is not as frightening as it appears to be. To be effective on your job-seeking quest, you need a good strategy, a clear mind, a strong sense of determination, and sometimes a bit of luck, like Emilio's story – just like real hunting!

Let us look at some tactics you can employ in your job-searching quest.

MAP OUT YOUR PLAN

Treat job-searching like a class project. You would only jump recklessly into a project with proper planning, would you? The best way to do this is by creating a timeline from the start of your job-searching plan until the end. It is an excellent way to track what you have done, how much you have done, and what you might have missed (refer to **Figure 6.3**). For example, you could start by dedicating a few days to using AI tools to create your résumé and cover letter, working on the finer points and polishing them up.

While working on those, you can research companies on your target list to find the right jobs to apply to. Then, once you have decided which jobs you are interested in, you should connect with employees at these companies and apply to the posted jobs within a fixed amount of time per day because it can get overwhelming if you are applying for jobs nonstop.

ESTABLISH YOURSELF ONLINE

Finding job opportunities has never been easier with the Internet. Many job posting sites allow you to create a profile with your professional details, a photograph of yourself (no selfies!), and a well-crafted résumé (visit your career center for assistance).

Applying for jobs on various platforms is as simple as clicking a button. Signing up for these websites allows them to constantly update you through your email, notifications, or alerts about the latest job opportunities suited to your interests—join their talent network. Often, job opportunities can be found within the depths of social media. That is right; you can still browse your favorite social networking site while simultaneously searching for job opportunities.

Use specific keywords when searching for jobs on social media for more accurate results. From the previous chapter, we learned that LinkedIn is the most commonly used social networking site for job-related services, while the more unconventional ones are Facebook, TikTok, and Instagram.

MAKING CONNECTIONS

In previous chapters, I mentioned the importance of networking events, networking opportunities, or just getting out there and networking with others. However, you must realize that networking skills are not necessarily taught in the classroom and do not come easy to many. Knowing how to network in college can mean the difference between finding a full-time job after graduation through your connections and scrambling to find one on your own. You never know that the person you meet may be the reason why you are starting a new job. In fact, 85% of hires result from personal connections.[40] That is why networking is so crucial.

STEVE JOBS' STORY

Fearless First Step

In a 1994 video interview with Steve Jobs, he points out that he never found anybody who didn't want to help him if he asked them for help.[41] Steve then tells a story about when he was in high school when he cold-called Hewlett-Packard's co-founder Bill Hewlett by finding his name in the phone book to request spare electronic parts. To his surprise, Bill Hewlett picked up the phone himself.

"He (Bill) laughed, and he gave me the spare parts to build the frequency counter, and he gave me a job that summer at Hewlett-Packard, working on the assembly line putting nuts and bolts together on frequency counters," Steve recalled. "He got me a job in the place that built them, and I was in heaven."

"I've never found anybody who said 'no' or hung up the phone when I called - I just asked," Steve continued. "Most people never pick up the phone and call. Most people never ask. And that is what separates sometimes the people who do things from the people who just dream about them. You gotta act and you gotta be willing to fail." Steve explained.

The interview ends with Steve Jobs giving some words of advice. "You've got to be willing to crash and burn, with people on the phone, with starting a company, with whatever," Steve said. "If you're afraid of failing, you won't get very far."

The internet obviously did not exist when Steve Jobs was 12 years old, but his story demonstrates how he took the initiative to research Bill Hewlett's number in the phone book and make a phone call. Steve had a clear purpose—asking for spare parts—and he made a favorable impression on Bill Hewlett, which led to a summer job.

This story about Steve Jobs illustrates the power of asking and the importance of making connections, also known as networking. Networking allows you to meet new people, learn about new opportunities, and get your name out there for potential possibilities.

Let's dive into some practical advice to help you start building your professional network while still in college.

CRAFT YOUR ELEVATOR PITCH

Once you have figured out your career goals, you can work on your elevator pitch — a summary of your professional history, your future plans, and what you can offer others. It is your quick, personal selling statement. This is the pitch you will use in conversation when trying to establish a connection with somebody, whether at a networking event or elsewhere.

There are quite a few resources to develop your elevator pitch. If you are not sure how to start, I recommend visiting your career center for assistance and support first. In the meantime, here are a few suggestions to include in your one-minute pitch:

1. **Who are you?** Your name and something that differentiates you from your peers (e.g. major/degree, athlete, veteran) and/or establishes a relationship (graduate of the same college, from the same hometown, etc.).

2. **Your specific goal/career interest**. This will allow that person to help or connect you to someone who can.

3. **How have you demonstrated your interest?** Demonstrate your interest and experience in the field with examples of things you have already completed. Don't just say, "I have always wanted to be a software engineer," but instead, "I have taken computer science courses and volunteered at a coding for kid organization".

4. **Why are you qualified?** Demonstrate your qualifications by sharing leadership and work experience, achievements, expertise, skills, and strengths.

5. **A question or request for assistance.** Consider giving the person two options for ways they may be of assistance. For example, "If your company offers internships, I would appreciate the name of the person in charge of that program, or perhaps I could meet with you in person to learn more about your organization and opportunities in the marketing profession." Be sure to offer each contact your business card or use your LinkedIn QR code to connect for future reference.

You might also benefit from brainstorming conversation starter topics or networking questions, such as what kind of advice they might offer to someone new to their industry.

INTRODUCE YOURSELF AT EVENTS

Colleges seem to organize an abundance of social events each week for students, faculty, and alums. Go online and find a copy of your school's events calendar, and look for opportunities to meet alums, guest speakers, and campus recruiters.

At an event, whether a career fair or a roundtable discussion, consider approaching someone you want to develop a professional connection with and introducing yourself. This might be intimidating, but it is an essential part of networking. The more you practice introducing yourself at events, the more confidence you build.

JOIN A CLUB

Universities typically feature lengthy lists of clubs and activities for learners to join. Choose one that is enjoyable for you and allows you to connect with other students, club alums, and advisors (often professors). On-campus groups will enable you to make new connections with your peers from various majors and practice team-building and other networking skills.

Networking also allows you to hone your soft skills. The more you practice networking, the more you can strengthen your interpersonal and communication skills while building your confidence to stand out to future employers.

MEET EMPLOYERS FACE-TO-FACE

Keep a look out for career fairs and try to attend as many as possible. If you are still in college, look for career visits or talks organized by your career center (see Chapter 4). In addition to handing out your résumé to company representatives while they are on campus, you will also have great hands-on experience meeting with employers from different organizations.

With all the advancements in technology today, remember that people still hire people, so this is a great opportunity to make an in-person impression. Plus, it helps narrow down your options into specific fields. Remember to bring copies of your résumé with you—it shows determination!

Before attending job fairs or career visits, remember to research the companies that will be present on those days. Narrow down your options to companies you are interested in, and find out what kind of organization they are, whether they are hiring, and if you match the criteria for their job openings.

KEEP IN TOUCH WITH YOUR CONNECTIONS

Remember to network! This includes previous guest speakers or lecturers, classmates, colleagues, and mentors. Keep up a good rapport with them, as this will make them more likely to share opportunities with you or even refer you to jobs you are currently searching for. You must continuously expand your network circle beyond friends and family to collect as much information about opportunities you discover or intend to apply for.

LinkedIn is a great way to network. Establishing yourself on this platform should be one of the first steps to start your job search. You will be able to make and maintain connections, and employers will also be able to see how well-connected you are with others. Your connections can also endorse the skills you listed on your profile, which gives you more credibility, as discussed in Chapter 9.

How do you expand your network strategically? I would not just start clicking on people's LinkedIn profiles to connect. Instead, I would reach out to the following profiles:

- People you have something in common with (e.g. shared background, affiliation, club or organization).

- People who may have had a similar internship that you had or wish to have, and they are now full-time employees.

- People who are alumni and have established professional careers.

- People who have a job or work at a company that interests you.

- People who may be able to connect you to someone who can help you achieve your goals. •

- People connected to other members you know.

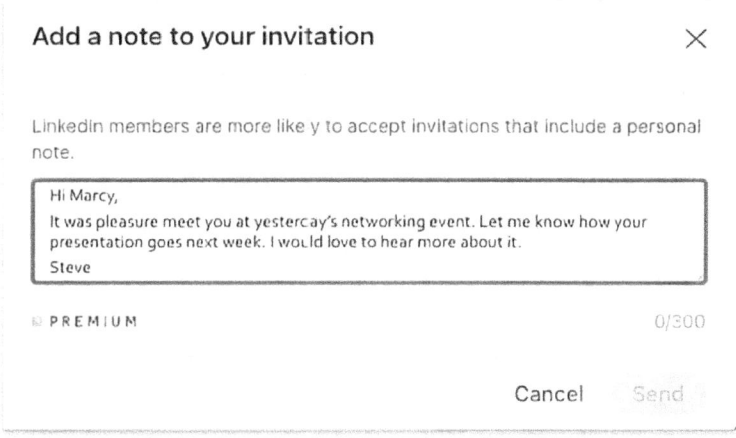

Figure 10.1: LinkedIn Invitation Note

What should you say? Always personalize your connection request. After clicking "Connect" on someone's LinkedIn profile, be sure to select "Add a note" (see **Figure 10.1**). This short message is your first opportunity to start a conversation and give the person a reason to accept your invitation. If the person accepts, your customized note will appear in their LinkedIn inbox—so make it count.

Here are a few practical tips to guide your outreach:

- **Keep it concise**: Aim for 2–3 sentences. Remember, you're limited to 200 characters on the Free Plan and 300 on the Premium Plan.
- **Make it personal**: Consider including—
  - Who you are
  - How you came across their profile
  - Why you want to connect

People will often preview your profile before deciding whether to accept your invite. That's why it's critical to ensure your LinkedIn profile is complete and professional—something we already covered in Chapter 9. Your profile should have a clear photo, showcase your interests and qualifications, and reflect your career goals. Let your personality shine a bit, too—this helps you stand out.

You may occasionally get a message like:

- "I'm honored by the invitation, but why do you want to connect?"
- "Sorry, where did we meet again?"
- "Thanks—but how would this connection be helpful?"

Don't take these personally. These responses are natural when someone is being selective or just unsure.

Do's:

1. Mention people you both know (if relevant)
2. Reference how you've met, if applicable (e.g., at a conference)
3. Give a simple reason for connecting without oversharing—leave room for curiosity
4. Show interest in staying connected

5. Reinforce that connecting is always a win-win

Don'ts:

- Launch into a sales pitch
- Send a generic message without personalization
- Lie about how you know someone—honesty builds trust
- Use tired clichés ("Let's connect and grow our networks!")

Interestingly, some studies suggest that neutral requests—those that are polite but not overly detailed—often get higher acceptance rates. But every connection is different. Try out different approaches and see what works best for you.

The key is to be respectful, curious, and genuine. Even if someone doesn't respond right away, don't be discouraged. Professionals are busy, and some may not check their invitations often. Be patient.

In the long run, your network can offer incredible value—career insights, résumé feedback, referrals, or even mentorship. One thoughtful message today could lead to an opportunity tomorrow.

AN INSIDER'S VIEW

As a Talent Acquisition Executive at a data startup company, I receive many daily LinkedIn invites from Sales Development Representatives looking to sell me something, vendors wanting to offer their services, and job seekers exploring opportunities. While I am a big believer in networking, these requests often feel like cold calls since they come from strangers. As a result, I am very selective about whom I accept and engage with. Like many other professionals who receive LinkedIn invites, I review the sender's profile to determine if there is a compelling reason to accept or reject the request to connect.

When you get as many LinkedIn requests as I do, try to put yourself in my shoes when you receive an invitation to connect as to wonder: why does someone want to connect with you without ever "meeting" you? If you receive an invitation to connect with no note, then you wonder why they did not even have the courtesy to include a customized note clarifying why they want to connect. Maybe they offer a note, but it is one of those *"we have a lot of connections in common, and we are in the same industry, so let's connect"* notes. Really, is this all you have got?

If a stranger wants to connect, I expect a note that provides a reason or some context. Don't get me wrong; I am open to connecting with new people, but I believe in putting in the effort to develop a coherent and relevant reason for the connection. Otherwise, like many other professionals, I may not respond or accept.

Here are a few real examples of connection requests and notes added to invitations that caught my attention:

> *"Hi Ed, I'm a sophomore studying Computer Science. I know it may be early for internships, but I noticed that your company hired a few last summer. I'd like to connect with you or someone from the engineering team to learn more about what your company tends to look for when hiring interns. Thank you."*
> (300/300)

This example speaks for itself. The college student used every character available when writing this note, demonstrating authenticity, specificity, and intentionality in her message. She also showed that she had done research about the company and its past internships, personalizing the note effectively.

> *"Hi Ed, I see on your LI profile that you once interned at (company) and have done a nice job with your career progression. I'm reaching out to professionals like yourself so I can learn what helped you make a successful*

transition. I'd love to connect and learn more about your career path."
(290/300)

It is personal. It is genuine. It is real. The message is direct with some pleasantries, and I know upfront that this is a coaching discussion.

> *"Hi Ed, I was at the "Women in Revenue" event, and I appreciate the insights you gave on the panel. I'm a junior student majoring in business and I'm seeking an internship to give me more exposure to Sales. I'd love to pick your brain to see what career paths I can pursue. Can we connect? (name)"*
> *(299/300)*

This is the type of note where I'm most likely to accept a connection request. When someone takes the time to state how they found me and their purpose for reaching out, there's no guessing involved. It clearly shows the genuine interest of the person wanting to connect. This leads to a conversation I am willing to have as a next step.

As you can see, there is a right and wrong way to "add a note" to a connection request on LinkedIn. Here are a few examples of what NOT to say when adding a note to a connection request:

> *"Hi Edward! I'm expanding my LinkedIn professional network and would like to add you to my connections. Thank you!" (114/300)*

This example feels like an automated LinkedIn outreach message. When I receive a non-personalized note like this, it raises a red flag. My first reaction is, "What does this person want from me?" If I accept this invitation, will they try to sell me something? If I am left guessing the motive, I tend to reject the invitation. So, avoid these types of messages as they decrease the odds of connecting with someone you are targeting.

> *"Hi Mr. Avila, I'm looking for an entry-level position at your company. I'm attaching my résumé for your review. Please let me know if you'd be open to a conversation to discuss any open positions that I may be a fit. Best regards, (name)" (239/300)*

At first glance, this message seems fine. Most of us in Talent Acquisition have received such connection requests with notes like this example. However, if you read it closely, it is very generic. The college student did not put much effort into researching the company or explaining which role they are interested in and why. He is leaving it to me to review his résumé and decide if he would be a match for a role, I may not even have open—this is not my job!

The more you leave it to someone else to determine if there is a potential match, the less likely you are to get an acceptance of your connection request.

There are many opinions about whether you should include a note in LinkedIn connection requests. The message you send alongside your connection request can significantly affect your acceptance rate. Writing a customized note in a text field that only allows 300 characters takes just two minutes.

A thoughtful message can build rapport with a stranger and be the first step in developing a long-lasting relationship. A highly personalized message might be far more effective for your audience than no message at all. Still not convinced. Ask yourself, *"Do you really want to connect with someone if they don't think you are worth that two-minute investment?"*

Let's Recap!

- Think of job hunting as a quest, it takes several approaches, methods and actions to enter the job market. It is not just sending out applications and waiting for that elusive response, it takes more effort.

- As tough job hunting might seem, it is important to keep your chin up, continue to move forward, and stay positive.

- There is no better place to start networking than college! That is where most people make lasting friendships, discover themselves, and determine their career paths.

- By forging strong connections with other students, professors, and advisors, they can open doors that make launching a career easier.

- Personalized LinkedIn notes can improve your chances of having your LinkedIn connection requests accepted and build an awesome network!

CHAPTER 10: QUEST? I'M ALREADY ON A QUEST

Key Takeaways

NOTES:_____

_____

_____

_____

_____

_____

_____

ACTIONS:_____

_____

_____

_____

_____

_____

_____

11

CHAPTER

ONCE UPON A TIME

D o you recall, as a child, being introduced to storytelling by your mom, dad, or teacher? Whether it was at bedtime or after recess at school, they would tell or read you captivating stories that grabbed your attention, drew you into the narrative, and created memorable experiences. Children love to hear a good story from babyhood to the early teens.

Well, storytelling is not just for children. Successful presenters, public speakers, salespeople, and politicians have mastered the art of storytelling. They typically use personal experiences and relatable analogies to tie up their main points. The personal story makes them more excited and transfers their passion to the audience. A great tale demands just the right amount of detail—no more and no less.

As a job seeker, you should use storytelling, too. It can be a powerful tool that helps you leave a lasting impression on hiring managers. We tend to remember stories longer and better than facts on a résumé or LinkedIn profile.

MY STORY

Power of Storytelling

I attended an *HR Symposium* in the Bay Area several years ago. This annual conference brings together business experts, leaders, and human resources professionals to discuss issues and trends affecting Human Resources and Silicon Valley across all industries. There was a panel of distinguished HR leaders from various companies. I have attended many conferences over the last decade, but this one was unique.

The panelists discussed the "art of storytelling," sharing their experiences with recent projects and how they formulated solutions to overcome challenges in a dynamic business and economic environment. They shared personal stories about failures and real-life learnings.

The art of storytelling provides vivid details that help an audience visualize what is being presented, influencing and stimulating an emotional reaction. It engages an audience more deeply than merely exchanging facts, data, or statistics. Needless to say, the session was informative. It was not just another boring conference; it was meaningful, inspiring, and engaging. It reminded me that facts alone don't move people—stories do. And if I wanted to inspire action in my career, I needed to be more intentional about how I shared mine.

As a job seeker, the stories you must be ready to tell during a job interview are about your unique experiences in previous jobs, classroom assignments, or group projects - things that back up the skills and qualifications you wrote about on your résumé or LinkedIn profile. It is a way of telling authentic details about yourself that leaves a lasting impression with interviewers. This method allows interviewers to see you as an individual, which is critical to standing out among other candidates.[42] Stories enable job seekers to show competence and transferable skills to the job opportunities.

Storytelling is a skill that can be learned, and it is quite effective in a résumé based on your experiences. As a candidate, you can weave stories into the discussion when you talk about your accomplishments and significant achievements. We all have stories to tell, and some of these are your favorites that you tend to share with your closest friends on a regular basis. Stories provide an engaging narrative of what happened, whether you have overcome an obstacle, completed a significant task, or learned from a mistake.

If you recently completed a summer internship, integrate insights from this experience into your storytelling and rehearse it aloud, either in person or virtually, with classmates and peers. This preparation will enhance your ability to discuss your work experience fluently, illustrating how it aligns with your field of study through real-world examples. By doing so, you can effectively articulate why you are well-suited for the current role.

Crafting a personal narrative can significantly boost your confidence in interviews. It allows you to highlight your most relevant skills and connect them directly to the role you're applying for. When you view the interview as an opportunity to tell your story—clearly, concisely, and with purpose—it not only reduces stress, but also makes the conversation more engaging. And in many cases, it can be the key to landing the internship or job.

LARRY'S STORY

Beyond the Résumé

Larry, a seasoned technical recruiter with over a decade of experience in cybersecurity, specializes in senior technical roles and is often the go-to recruiter for entry-level engineers at his company. With job postings attracting hundreds of applicants, many from top technical universities across the US, Larry explains, "Cybersecurity remains a high-demand sector due to ongoing data and infrastructure threats, making it a popular career choice for students who want to start a career in this sector."

Given the overwhelming volume of résumés received through their career page, Larry outlines the initial screening criteria: "We prioritize résumés, unofficial college transcripts including GPA, and cover letters." He emphasizes that while experience, skills, and general education are valued by many hiring managers, some also consider specific courses taken as part of the degree program to gain a broader perspective on applicants' qualifications, which aids in narrowing down the candidate pool.

Larry points out a common challenge faced with engineering students: "Many have impressive résumés based on coursework and class projects but lack relevant experience." To assess candidates, his team evaluates both technical competence and essential non-technical skills such as communication, curiosity, critical thinking, teamwork, and collaboration. "Communication skills are crucial," Larry notes, "as new graduates must effectively communicate across different levels within an organization."

Larry stresses the importance of candidates' ability to articulate their thought processes during interviews: "It's surprising how many struggle to explain their approach to coding tasks or understanding of problem statements." He advises applicants to use the S.T.A.R. model effectively, emphasizing the significance of including the 'why' in their situational examples. "Telling a story can be surprisingly difficult to tell. Your story might include a class project, which was unexpectedly delayed, a classmate you have a history of conflict with or a tough professor that you found a challenge understanding the complex material," Larry expands. "These are all potential stories of situations where you can demonstrate your abilities. If you know the reason why, explain it. It's a core element of the situation."

"We interview lots of smart graduates. The best stories are the ones where students can describe how they strategically overcame a challenge or problem and have quantifiable data to back it up. I am looking for curiosity, perseverance, determination, and critical thinking themes.

The interview process is over if they cannot go beyond their technical capabilities and communicate their interests, experiences or even explain what was accomplished in past class projects." Larry concludes.

⚲AN INSIDER'S VIEW ⚲

Who doesn't love a good story? And now you have one to tell. Here are three tips to help you be a good storyteller at your following job interview:

1. **Behavioral Interviewing:** Have you ever been asked to tell a story in an interview? In response to something like, "Tell me about a situation where you faced a challenge in a previous position and how you handled it." This type of interview question invites you to tell your story. One of the biggest mistakes candidates make during an interview is that the candidate answers

the interviewer's questions with simple facts and details. Or they talk about the intellectual way they would solve a problem.

This style and approach to storytelling are powerful tools for job seekers. Telling a story structurally is an effective way to describe events in your past and how these events demonstrate your talents and skills. It also effectively describes how you would approach future situations relevant to the job.

2. **Memorable Stories:** Great stories include sufficient details (think about how an engaging novel describes the environment so you can picture yourself in action). Details create a memorable story and help the interviewer visualize what you are trying to illustrate. Since hiring managers have plenty of suitable candidates to choose from, expect them to ask more challenging interview questions as they try to reduce candidate pools and ensure they hire the right people. Well-told stories leave memorable impressions that convince potential employers that the job candidate has the skills to succeed.

   Be careful how you showcase the skills and abilities highlighted on your résumé or LinkedIn profile. For every little thing you highlight as a significant achievement, make sure you have at least one prepared story that can support it. For example, if you write in your professional summary that you have a "strong record of meeting critical project deadlines despite unforeseen obstacles," be ready for the hiring manager to ask you a behavioral question like: "Tell me about a time you encountered an unforeseen obstacle. What did you do to overcome it?".

3. **Drama Sells:** The most memorable movies and novels have content that is either out of the ordinary or contains a bit of

drama. Our brain remembers drama or anything that stimulates it. While you communicate your solution to a problem, you should seek ways to respond in a way that will engage the interviewer. Like all great stories, ensure you have clear context and link back to the original question, so it resonates with your interviewer.

The biggest mistake candidates make is spending more time on writing their résumé rather than preparing for the job interview. Most people spend an average of ten or more hours writing or changing their résumé and only one hour preparing for the interview. Some job seekers even spend hundreds of dollars on résumé writing services but still only spend an average of an hour preparing for the only event that can get them hired – the interview. If you spend time preparing for each interview, this investment alone will improve your outcome of finding and landing your next internship or first job.

If you are not a natural storyteller, start practicing. Tell your unique story using the following S.O.A.R (see **Figure 11.1**) structure: beginning, middle, and end. Do not just write it; recite it and memorize it. Make your stories relevant and tie them to the job. The job interview is the most important moment in your job search. Your résumé may get you to the interview, but only your job interview skills will secure the job offer.

- **SITUATION:** What was the problem or opportunity? (Start of "WHAT" was going on at the time?)

- **OBJECTIVE:** What was the objective or desired outcome? (Rest of "WHAT" was going on?)

- **ACTION:** What action did you take? ("HOW" did you approach the situation?)

- **RESULTS:** What was the result or impact? ("WOW!" What happened?) Try to quantify.

Figure 11.1: S.O.A.R. Framework

Remember these three tips the next time a hiring manager asks you a question during a job interview. You have amazing stories to tell, so do not sell yourself short when allowed to highlight your experience. The S.O.A.R. framework should enhance your ability to explain yourself more powerfully and memorably.[43] Rehearse to ensure you nail the delivery of telling these developed stories out loud a few times, and you will be well on your way to acing your following job interview.

🐂 Let's Be Bullish:

Chapter 7 covered the importance of reflecting on your strengths and interests and how that would align with possible career paths. As a next step, use your college experience and insights about yourself to flush out some of your key accomplishments. As you reflect on these significant milestones, think about those things you are most proud of and then review how you can use this information to tell your unique story that would differentiate you as a leading candidate. To help you with this process, you can use the S.O.A.R. method.

To break it down, S.O.A.R. is an acronym for Situation, Obstacle, Objective or Task, Action, and Result. This method is similar to the S.T.A.R. method previously mentioned in Chapter 8. By understanding and practicing this method, you can effectively demonstrate your strengths and align them with the company's desired behaviors, values, and traits when asked behavioral-based job interview questions.

Helping college students become articulate and persuasive on the fly is extremely difficult - using the S.O.A.R. The Storytelling worksheet (see **Figure 11.2**) prompts can help you write your success stories well-structured. It can also help you avoid forgetting some critical context or prevent you from rambling when responding to the interviewer's questions. As you identify various stories from your unique background, include the strengths/skills you demonstrated (hard and soft skills) and note where the accomplishment occurred so you can refer to these as you practice. Practice articulating your stories using the S.O.A.R format before the interview, ensuring clarity and conciseness in your responses.

Until you gain the confidence to convey that you are truly a qualified candidate for the role, the S.O.A.R method will help you identify stories that can be used in interviewing with Talent Acquisition Partners and hiring managers.

Situation / Opportunity (Start of "WHAT")	
Objective / Desired Outcome (Rest of "WHAT")	
Actions Taken ("HOW")	
Results & Impact (WOW!")	
Strengths / Skills Demonstrated	
Where This Happened	
Is it highlighted on résumé?	

Figure 11.2: S.O.A.R Storytelling Worksheet

Ultimately, I recommend preparing 10-15 distinct success stories to cover as many different types of questions as you may be asked in an interview. If prepared, you can extract developed stories from your mental inventory rather than drawing a blank or struggling to answer interview questions.

Believe me, you have valuable stories to tell. If you were involved in organizations and clubs on campus or volunteered for philanthropic activities, these all count as experience. By using the S.O.A.R. method, you can articulate your skills and accomplishments clearly, making a strong impression on potential employers. Over time, mastering this method will become second nature as you navigate your career path and pursue future opportunities.

For further guidance or feedback on mastering the S.O.A.R. technique, consider visiting your career center—they're equipped to provide valuable support.

Let's Recap!

- Stories stick—interviewers will remember a great story over bullet points any day.

- Use the S.O.A.R. method (Situation, Obstacle, Action, Result) to structure your responses.

- Practice telling stories about your experiences that highlight specific skills and outcomes.

- Prepare a mental library of 10–15 stories so you're never caught off guard.

- Great storytellers get hired. Learn the art, and your confidence will shine through.

CHAPTER 11: ONCE UPON A TIME

Key Takeaways

NOTES:_____

_____

_____

_____

_____

_____

_____

ACTIONS:_____

_____

_____

_____

_____

_____

_____

12

CHAPTER

BLURRY VISION (NO MORE)

I t's not just a job search — it's your strategy. If you're a college student trying to break into the workforce, chances are you've heard the usual advice: *"Start early. Network. Tailor your résumé. Apply to lots of jobs."*

And while that advice isn't wrong, let's be honest—it often leads to confusion, frustration, and burnout.

That's where the **Bullish Career Canvas™** comes in (see **Figure 12.1**).

Inspired by the Lean Canvas model used by startups to build business plans, this one-page tool helps you map out your personal career strategy with clarity and intention.[44] You don't need a business idea. You are the business. Your skills, story, and strategy are what you're building. This canvas helps you define where you are, what you want, and how to close the gap.

In the startup world, founders use the Lean Canvas to test assumptions, identify customers, and refine their plan. In your world—the job seeker's world—the Bullish Canvas does the same: It helps you organize your thoughts, identify target employers, clarify your unique value, and take focused, strategic action.

AIDA'S STORY

The Pivot

Aida was a senior Environmental Studies major who showed up to the career center that I was volunteering at in full panic mode. Graduation is a semester away. She had no leads, no résumé, no idea where to start.

As I began to work with her in our first 1-on-1 session, I introduced her to a blank Bullish Career Canvas and said, *"Let's stop guessing. Let's map it."*

Aida was very process-oriented, and she immediately felt comfortable with the framework. She took the tool home to review it and returned for our next Zoom call with a list of thoughtful questions.

We began filling in the canvas together:

- **Problem:** She didn't know where to apply.
- **Targeted Employers:** Environmental nonprofits and green tech firms.
- **Unique value proposition?** As president of our campus sustainability task force, I led three successful campaigns to reduce plastics—combining hands-on leadership with data-driven impact.
- **Available Resources:** Career center workshops; alumni mentors in EnvironTech club; free Tableau course

- **Support Channels:** Sustainability faculty advisor; LinkedIn alumni network; campus green-jobs Slack group
- **Key Metrics:** 10 outreach messages; 5 tailored applications; one-page portfolio by spring break
- **Success Indicators**: 3 informational interviews; 2 internship offers; portfolio live by April
- **Continuous Learning:** Complete Tableau basics by March; publish portfolio mini case on department website.

Within weeks, Aida had more clarity than ever before—and just two months later, she accepted an internship where she helped establish her company's Corporate Sustainability Program. Her role involved gathering and measuring environmental data to align initiatives with corporate goals.

AN INSIDER'S VIEW

What This Canvas Reveals I've interviewed thousands of candidates over the years. The ones who stand out aren't always the ones with perfect GPAs or fancy degrees. They're the ones who know:

- What they want
- What they offer
- And how to tell their story

That's exactly what the Bullish Career Canvas helps you do. It transforms your swirling thoughts into a structured plan of action.

CHALLENGE(S)
What's blocking your progress right now? (e.g. no clarity, lack of confidence, no experience

DESIRED ROLE(S)
What job roles or functions are you aiming for?

ESSENTIAL SKILLS + CAREER VALUES
What skills (hard & soft) are required for these roles? What values are important to you in a job for you to thrive?

UNIQUE VALUE PROPOSITION + THE PITCH
What makes you worth hiring? What's your personal "wow" factor? Can you describe your story in 2-3 sentences?

SKILL/EXPERIENCE GAPS
What are you missing today? What's holding you back from being competitive?

STRATEGIC ACTIONS
What steps will you take now? (e.g. Update résumé, network, take a course, etc.)

AVAILABLE RESOURCES
What career center services, courses, professors, platforms, or mentors can you use?

TARGETED COMPANIES/ SECTORS
What industries or employers are you focusing on? Do your skills align with these companies?

SUPPORT CHANNELS
Who can offer guidance and support? (e.g. Alumni, advisors, professors, former coworkers, friends, etc.)

CONTINUOUS LEARNING
How will you keep expanding your knowledge and skills?

SUCCESS INDICATORS
What does success look like for you? (e.g. Finding a mentor, securing an internship, building a portfolio)

KEY METRICS
How will you measure your progress? (e.g. Applications submitted, interviews? New reach outs?

Figure 12.1: Bullish Career Canvas™

A PRACTICAL TOOL: Bullish Career Canvas™

The Bullish Career Canvas™ is a strategic career readiness tool designed to help job seekers create a clear and actionable plan. It's organized into key blocks, each addressing a critical aspect of job search planning.

Here's how each section of the Bullish Career Canvas helps you take control of your career path:

Canvas Section	Career Readiness Focus
Challenge	What's your biggest career obstacle right now? *(Lack of clarity? No experience? Imposter syndrome?)*
Desired Role(s)	Which job titles, industries, or functions are you targeting? Be 1–2 specific roles.
Unique Value Proposition (Elevator Pitch/Story)	Describe your personal brand in 2–3 confident sentences. What makes you worth hiring?
Essential Skills (+ Career Values)	List your technical & soft skills—and the workplace environments in which you thrive (structure? autonomy? mission-driven?).
Skill/Experience Gaps	What skills, experiences, or credentials are you missing?
Strategic Actions	What concrete steps will address your top challenge? *(Network, upskill, update LinkedIn, etc.)*
Available Resources	What people, programs, or platforms can help you close those gaps? *(Career center, professors, online courses, etc.)*
Targeted Companies/Sectors	Which organizations or sectors are most likely to value your skills?

Support Channels	How will you build relationships? *(Alumni network, LinkedIn groups, faculty mentors, peer advisors, etc.)*
Success Indicators	What does "career ready" look like in 3–6 months? *(Internship secured? Portfolio live? 3 callbacks?)*
Key Metrics	How will you track progress? *(Apps submitted per week, outreach messages sent, interviews scheduled)*
Continuous Learning	Which courses, certifications, or projects will you pursue next? *(E-learning, workshop series, pro bono project)*

A LIVING STRATEGY, NOT A ONE-TIME EXERCISE

The Bullish Career Canvas isn't just a worksheet. It's a dynamic, evolving tool.

- Revisit it after each semester, internship, new class, or even a rejection—it's your checkpoint.
- It helps you make better decisions by encouraging you to think holistically, not reactively.
- Use it to track patterns, test new ideas, and adjust your strategy in real time.
- It becomes a conversation starter and communication tool you can confidently share with mentors, professors, or career advisors to get tailored feedback.

When used consistently, the Canvas becomes more than a planning tool—it becomes your personal dashboard for intentional growth.

🐂 Let's Be Bullish:

The canvas isn't about having all the answers. It's about organizing what you *do* know, spotting what's missing, and gaining momentum.

This tool will help you:

- Stop aimlessly applying and start applying with purpose
- Track what's working (and what's not)
- Speak confidently about your value
- Stay focused through graduation stress and peer comparison

Let's Recap!

- The Bullish Career Canvas™ is your personal blueprint to move from confusion to clarity.

- Don't guess—map it. Identify your challenges, goals, skills, gaps, and support network.

- Revisit and revise your canvas frequently. It's a living tool, not a one-time exercise.

- Confidence comes from clarity—and clarity comes from structured thinking.

- Use your Canvas as your compass—and your confidence will follow.

CHAPTER 12: BLURRY VISION (NO MORE)

Key Takeaways

NOTES:_____

_____

_____

_____

_____

_____

_____

ACTIONS:_____

_____

_____

_____

_____

_____

_____

13

CHAPTER

PULLING IT ALL TOGETHER

Congratulations on reaching the final chapter. As you've read throughout this book, you may have noticed that I didn't delve deeply into crafting résumés, cover letters, interview preparation, or writing follow-up thank-you notes. Instead, I believe these topics would be better served by leveraging AI tools like ChatGPT or Gemini and working closely with your university's career center counselors or peer advisors. These resources could provide you with more guidance than I ever could.

Despite that, my intent with this book is to give you as many insights from a recruiter's perspective as possible. The strategies written in these chapters are to empower you for a successful job search and better equip you with advice, tips, and tools to enter the job market. Hopefully, I was able to accomplish that with my personal experiences and stories; however, I am not ready to wrap this up.

Your college experience offers a special place to expand your academic learning, explore your passions, and delve deep into your sense of self. Your college years are a time for self-discovery and personal growth. Believe it or not, this personal growth will continue as you enter the next phase of your career and embark on your professional journey.

TURNING REJECTIONS INTO OPPORTUNITIES

Let's talk about rejections—a significant part of your job search journey. Remember back to when you were a high school senior, eagerly awaiting college decisions? As a parent, I witnessed firsthand the stress and anticipation my son experienced during that long wait. I'm sure you can relate—it was tough. The disappointment of receiving a "deferral" or a "rejection" from one of your top college choices can be disheartening. It feels like a setback.

But here's the thing—it's not the end of the road. Life has a way of unfolding as it's meant to. Just like my son eventually found the right fit and is thriving at his chosen university, you too will find your path. Rejections, whether from colleges or job applications, are part of the journey towards discovering the opportunities that align best with your goals and aspirations. So, while it may sting initially, remember that each rejection is a steppingstone towards finding the right opportunity for you. Keep pushing forward with determination and resilience—you're on your way to achieving great things.

Do not let rejection from your job searches get you down—it is just part of the interviewing process. While this lesson in rejection may cut deep, it is very likely that you will encounter this type of scenario again in life. I guess I can say that it is good practice. How you handle rejection now will help you better approach potentially being rejected from other life experiences, like job opportunities. Let me explain.

Regarding your job searches, it is like when you were waiting for college admission decisions. Rejections are not the end of the road. It is part of your journey towards career readiness success. Use rejection to your advantage. Think of rejection as instant feedback on your interview performance. Every "no" from a potential employer will give some insight *– Was it your résumé? Was it your interview skills? Was it your body language? Did you lack chemistry with the interviewer? Did you research enough about the company? Do you ask good questions? Was it your delivery?* Treat each rejection as a data point to refine your approach. It offers an opportunity to learn and improve.

You can identify data, such as patterns, by analyzing constructive rejection feedback. That way, you can adapt and make the necessary changes for the next one—remember the key points in Chapter 6, which talks about having a more data-driven mindset.

Take the time to reflect on this vital insight: when faced with rejection during your job search, avoid placing blame on the interview process, the applicant tracking system, or others. Instead, focus on understanding how you can enhance your performance for future interactions, whether it's an initial call with a recruiter, an interview with a hiring manager, or a panel discussion with a selection team.

Failing to secure the job doesn't define your success. It simply indicates that your current approach didn't yield the desired outcome. Rejection offers immediate feedback and valuable lessons. Take responsibility for what you can learn and influence. While it's tempting to attribute setbacks to external factors like the ATS system, the "black hole" job market, or even the recruiter, true empowerment comes from concentrating on what you can personally manage and control.

It is ok to request and ask for feedback after a job rejection so you can improve. While not all companies offer it, as it can be awkward or uncomfortable, it's worth overcoming any hesitation. If you do gather the courage to request feedback and the opportunity arises, here are a few key points to keep in mind:

- Be polite and listen.
- Don't get defensive.
- Don't try to argue or disagree with the criticism.
- Don't try to change their decision.
- Stay positive and express gratitude for being open and honest with the feedback.
- Ask if you can stay in touch for future opportunities.

If the feedback data shows that you lack certain areas, develop an action plan to help you acquire these capabilities - tailor your résumé, get better at interviewing, do more research on the company (or product), or improve your storytelling. Consider reviewing the job description and ask yourself if you can genuinely envision yourself in that role every day. If certain aspects didn't excite you, the interviewer might have sensed this as well. Take control of your job search process to adjust and move forward effectively.

After each rejection, take a step back and reflect on what went right and wrong. Most importantly, seek ways to adjust your approach. Interviewing is about evolving your strategy based on real-time feedback. You want to avoid repeating the same steps and expect different results. Turning rejections into opportunities for growth will transform your job search from a disheartening experience into a constructive journey.[45]

You may never know what results come from your actions. A great story may be ready to be told during your next interview. Imagine the next time you are asked by an interviewer, *"Tell me a time when you received criticism from*

221

others. How did you react to that criticism? Did you make improvements?" You should be prepared to give a real-life example where you discovered something about yourself and learned by adapting to feedback. So, embrace each "no" as a step closer to your "yes."

As you hone your interviewing skills, you'll come to understand that the journey to your ideal internship or first job isn't a straightforward path. It involves continuous learning and adaptation as you begin your professional career, with your trajectory being uniquely yours. Remember, everything happens for a reason. Rejection in job seeking doesn't define you—it's part of a purposeful journey. Your college experience shapes who you become, guiding you towards unexpected opportunities. Embrace the adventure and look forward to what lies ahead.

INSIGHTS FROM RECRUITERS

Throughout my career, I've had the privilege of collaborating with numerous outstanding recruiters from corporations, agencies, and staffing firms. Being part of an active network has connected me with a diverse community of peers who generously share their insights, resources, and experiences to foster mutual learning and advancement.

While writing this book, I frequently consulted with this community for their perspectives on career readiness. Many shared compelling stories about "common mistakes" or "red flags" they've encountered while interviewing college students. A job interview is akin to a crucial audition—it's your one opportunity to make a lasting impression and secure the position.

Here are insights compiled from recruiters on some of the most common mistakes candidates make, presented in no particular order:

"Not being prepared for an interview, period."

"Being a bit nervous is normal, but having a lack of passion, enthusiasm, or energy is something else."

"Many college students are not prepared for behavioral-based interviews - more practice please."

"Forgetting the details of the job description that they applied to."

"Being too comfortable when sharing a story."

"Forgetting what they wrote on their résumé." "Not researching the company and what we do."

"Not having real examples of accomplishments."

"Talking too much or cutting off the interviewer."

"Sharing too much personal information during the interview that is irrelevant to the job."

"Rambling - not focused enough; get to the point."

"Don't discuss personal topics or about certain individuals." "Embellishing past experiences."

"Not having questions to ask."

"Not listening to the questions being asked."

"Not being able to explain concisely what they want to do or why they are interviewing for the role."

"Not showing interest."

"Lacking confidence when speaking."

"Be careful not to be overconfident as this may come across as arrogance."

"Bad-mouthing others is pretty common when interviewing students; extremely unprofessional."

"Not answering questions directly."

"Poor body language during a Zoom interview."

"Having grammatical errors or typos on a résumé."

"Misspelled the company's name on a cover letter."

"Not making a great impression - what's their WOW factor?"

"Being too robotic with their pre-prepared responses."

"Not turning off your cell phone during the interview."

"Taking the job interview in a public location like a coffee shop - not a very suitable environment."

You'll come across plenty of blogs and articles detailing job interview blunders. The good news is that no one is perfect when it comes to interviewing, not even recruiters or hiring managers. Many common mistakes discussed in these pages can be avoided with research, preparation, and practice. You have insights from actual recruiters who have interviewed many college students before you; now, it's time for you to take proactive steps.

Merely understanding these pitfalls isn't sufficient. Take a critical look at the list and honestly assess which mistakes might apply to you. Self-awareness is key to maximizing your chances of a successful interview. Identify areas where you may struggle and if you're unsure about how to improve, seek guidance from your career counselor or peer advisor. They can offer valuable interviewing tips tailored to overcoming these common pitfalls, ultimately enhancing your prospects of securing the job.

Many of us need extra guidance and preparation to put our best foot forward and ace the job interview. **Figure 13.1** provides a framework for preparing for a 30-minute or 45-minute interview. The more you practice this structured flow, the more confident you will be and the better chance you will stand out as a memorable candidate. Focusing on these factors allows you to set yourself up for tremendous success and strengthen your candidacy in critical areas instead of falling victim to common mistakes recent graduates make.

HOW TO PREPARE FOR AN INTERVIEW

1. OPENING:

   o Create a strong first impression.

   o Build rapport with the interviewer/Be ready for the small talk (pleasantries).

   o Showcase your personality/Be friendly/Be polite.

2. BASIC ELEVATOR PITCH:

   o Tell me about yourself.

   o Strengths/Weaknesses/Key Differentiators.

3. COMPANY/ORGANIZATION:

   o Research the company, know the services or products, competitors, read recent press releases, under the values.

   o Why do you want to work here?

   o What value would you add?

4. BEHAVIORAL/ SITUATIONAL QUESTIONS:

   o Your Storytelling Bank (see **Figure 11.2**)

   o Align examples with skills required for the role; make the links.

5. QUESTIONS FOR INTERVIEWERS:

- o   Two to three thoughtful questions at the end of the interview.

- o   Panel - ask 1 question for each interviewer.

6.   CLOSING:

- o   What are the next steps?

- o   Reiterate your qualifications for the job.

- o   Emphasize your interest or passion for the position.

Figure 13.1: Interview Preparation Framework

🔍AN INSIDER'S VIEW 🔍

When my son was interviewing for a summer internship as a rising junior, he found himself navigating through multiple rounds of interviews, one after another, as part of the selection process. It was for an internship role that he was interviewing where the company attracted a staggering 300 applicants - that is a lot of candidates to go through just for one role, no joke.

In the first round, there was an initial call with a recruiter, then a second round with the hiring manager, a third round in which he was asked to work on a data set assignment, and a fourth round in which there was a panel with other team members. Ultimately, the fifth round was with the hiring manager and the recruiter, where they asked my son to jump on a Zoom call for a conversation. They finally extended the offer, and he accepted.

The whole interview process took my son approximately six weeks. It felt like a never-ending process, and that was just with one company. Between January and May, my son applied to more than 200 internship positions, and he interviewed with nine companies—each as grueling as the previous interview. *How many interviews are too many?*

My son's experience with a high number of interviews is far from unique. If you are going to start the interview process or are new to it, you must realize that most job interviews take time (see **Figure 13.2**). It is not something that companies rush through. Depending on the type of industry, the average hiring process may take 44 days to fill an open position (refer to **Chapter 6**).[46] Yes, the interview process can be frustrating and tiring. It is not a fast process, and it is not supposed to be easy. It is a "do not pass go, do not collect $200" moment.[47] While you may wish for faster responses from the company, it's crucial to accept that you have no control over this part of the process.

On TikTok, you'll find thousands of rant videos from users expressing their frustrations about the job-hunting process and saying how finding a well-paying job after graduation is nearly impossible. Here are a few rants captured:

"I'm so tired of it all. Going through job postings, speaking to recruiters, not getting a single reply..." ♡ 2867

"After companies ask for a sample of my work and then they ghost me. It makes me feel worthless..." ♡ 6351

"I graduated top of my class, and I can't even get a response back. I'm still working as a hostess at my part-time job. How am I expected to pay off my college loans..." ♡ 1804

"I went through three rounds of interviews, and I haven't heard back after three weeks. Hello, I'm perfect for the job..." ♡ 1393

These TikTokers are ranting about the difficulty of landing corporate jobs and hearing back from recruiters, and their struggles are real. I won't sugarcoat it; there's validity to these complaints. However, it's important to understand that a company's success heavily depends on its ability to attract and hire the right talent for their teams.

Interviewing candidates is a significant effort. If companies don't get it right, the consequences of a wrong hire can be severe, including losses in time, money, and productivity. Therefore, companies must take all reasonable steps to avoid hiring mistakes.

Recruiter Screen (30 min)	Hiring Manager (HM) (45-60 min)	Team Members (45 min each)	HM/Recruiter Close (45-60 min)
Goal	**Goal**	**Goal**	**Goal**
• Qualify the candidate. • Sell the company and the role. • Assess culture & team fit. • Obtain salary expectations. • Provide a summary of findings to the hiring manager.	• Identify any skill gaps. • Vet candidate based on assigned competencies. • If a fit, sell the opportunity - get him/her excited about the role. • May provide an assignment. • Provide candidate evaluation	• Each assigned Interviewer focuses on a specific area (technical or non-technical). • Assess culture & team fit. • Provide feedback and candidate evaluation. • Prepare for a debrief session.	• Based on debrief session: • If no, then send a "thanks, but no thanks" message via ATS. • If yes, then meet with the candidate to negotiate the details of an offer. • If the candidate accepts, then work on the onboarding process.

Figure 13.2: Example of an Interview Process

If you are waiting to hear back from a job interview, then remember the key points highlighted in **Chapter 8** of recommended actions that you can take to help you stand out as a candidate. If you're unsure about your next steps, check if you have an internal contact at the company you're interviewing with. Reach out to this person to see if they can advocate for your candidacy. Additionally, if you're hired, the employee may be eligible for a partial referral bonus, providing them with an incentive to help.

You can choose to wait and wonder, or you can create an action plan to follow up using various approaches covered in these chapters.

MAIA'S STORY

All In, Then Nothing

I worked with Maia during her senior year at an Ivy League university on the East Coast. She was determined to secure a Market Research role at a clinical-stage biotech company in Silicon Valley, aligning with the company's mission statement. Her résumé was impressive, showcasing summer internships at major pharmaceutical companies during her sophomore and junior years, which helped her develop the technical skills and experience needed for this type of work.

Maia was meticulous in her job applications, keeping track of all her targeted companies. She knew exactly how many résumés she sent out, who responded, and what was still pending. "I'm seeking a career where I can develop expertise in creating medicines to help people living with complex neurological disorders," she explained with a smile. I had no doubt she would find much success in this field.

As Maia started her final semester, she received a good response rate from her applications and secured five interviews in January. After a strong first interview, the second one stood out as her ideal job with her top-choice company. She described the team, the projects, and the Glassdoor reviews as 'perfect.' Excited, she canceled her remaining interviews to focus on this opportunity. The recruiter informed her that the team would decide within a week, so she stopped applying for other roles and waited.

When I checked in with Maia for an update, she texted, "One week passed with no news :(." She then received an update from the recruiter: "Sorry for the delay. We're running late with our decision, but you're still in the running." Two weeks later, she texted me, "Still no news - irritated." I suggested she review other roles on her tracker and refresh the list. By the end of February, she had followed up but had not heard back.

Maia remained hopeful but found it difficult to focus on other opportunities. She stalled her job search activities and tried various methods to connect with team members she had interviewed with, but received no response. A few weeks later, Maia received an email from the recruiter saying the position had been put "on hold" due to business reasons. Maia was devastated—not only because she wanted the role, but also because she had let other opportunities slip by while waiting. When we met on Zoom, she shared that she felt foolish and had to start over.

Maia went back into action mode. The challenge for her was that only a certain number of these entry-level roles were available in an already competitive industry. This meant revisiting the three companies she had canceled interviews with two months earlier, adding to her embarrassment.

Have you ever heard the saying, "Don't put all your eggs in one basket?" In simple terms, it means not relying on just one plan or resource for success because you could lose everything if it fails. Instead, having multiple options or investments is wise to spread the risk. As Maia experienced, don't apply for just one job and wait. Sometimes, job seekers stop or pause their job search entirely after interviewing for a job. This could be due to exhaustion from job hunting, the stress of the interview process, or a gut feeling that they are a 'shoe-in," as Maia felt.

Regardless, you must keep in mind that an interview is not a guarantee of a job, even if you feel that the job you applied for perfectly fits you. The reality is that if you have not been offered the position or started negotiations to accept it, you need to continue searching and interviewing for other opportunities.

No matter how confident you feel about a role, always keep moving forward and applying to other positions. If things work out, great. If they do not, you will be grateful you kept going.

Final Recap!

Throughout this book, I have provided you with data, knowledge, insights, and stories about job search strategies that you can implement as early as your freshman year through your senior year. Here is a quick recap of the book:

Part One, *"Yeah, I've Got Time,"* emphasizes that your four years at college will go by quickly, so start as early as possible when thinking about life after graduation.

- Chapter One focuses on self-discovery and leveraging resources available as you transition from home to the university.

- Chapter Two gives you a few examples of how you can develop a 360-degree view of learning what your values, strengths, and weaknesses are so you can begin to align them to possible career paths.

- Chapter Three expands on how you can develop skills through clubs, organizations, or volunteer work based on your interests beyond academics. It also introduces the concept of backward planning, which helps you break down the little steps on the path that enables you to move forward toward achieving the desired results.

Part Two, *"You've Got a Friend in Me,"* stresses that you are not alone on this career readiness journey and that you have people to support you.

- Chapter Four introduces how your career center at your university is an untapped resource for many students, and they can play a pivotal role in preparing you for the working world.

- Chapter Five encourages you to establish relationships with your professors. They can uniquely impact your academics and influence your future career.

- Chapter Six discusses the online job application "black hole." It takes you behind the scenes of the Talent Acquisition function so you can develop a data-driven mindset and make smarter job search decisions.

Part Three, *"You Ain't So Bad,"* expands your knowledge so that you can apply it to your job search strategies to reduce stress and anxiety. The more you learn, the more you realize that job hunting is not as difficult as it may seem.

- Chapter Seven provides an inside view of how companies plan for internships, allowing you to leverage this knowledge to gain a competitive advantage through strategic actions. It continues by breaking down the four stages of career readiness, starting with your first year.

- Chapter Eight provides a sneak peek behind the scenes and explains the Interview Debrief Sessions in depth. It also explains the differences between skills and competencies so that you can optimize your responses during an interview.

- Chapter Nine is all about LinkedIn, from setting up to boosting your profile. It examines the techniques and best practices of how Talent Acquisition professionals use LinkedIn Recruiter to find talent you can use to your advantage.

Part Four, *"Why So Serious?"* goes deeper to equip you with further knowledge so that you are more confident in your job search efforts, can enjoy it more, and do not take job hunting so seriously.

- Chapter Ten provides networking techniques both in person and on LinkedIn. It gives examples of effective ways to connect with new people.

- Chapter Eleven shows how you can stand out in interviews using personal storytelling and make your candidacy worth remembering. The storytelling approach lays the groundwork for applying portions of your experiences and skills to traditional interview questions.

- Chapter Twelve introduces the Bullish Career Canvas™, a one-page tool to map your career strategy. It helps you clarify your goals, target roles, unique value, and gaps—while outlining actions, resources, and support to move forward with confidence.

- Chapter Thirteen stresses how you can turn job rejections into your advantage. You can turn difficult situations into powerful learning experiences. It also emphasizes how preparation is critical to avoiding common mistakes and achieving career readiness.

CHAPTER 13: PULLING IT ALL TOGETHER

Key Takeaways

NOTES:_____

_____

_____

_____

_____

_____

_____

ACTIONS:_____

_____

_____

_____

_____

_____

_____

Pause & Reflect

Before You Close the Book – Go Make That Leap

You've come a long way—from confused and curious to focused and ready. You've seen how recruiters evaluate talent, how hiring really happens, and how to navigate the unwritten rules of career building. This wasn't fluff—this was a crash course in how hiring takes place behind the scenes in startup and corporate settings.

Take a moment to reflect:

- What part of your job search journey surprised you the most?

- What tools or strategies will you commit to using going forward?

- Are you now a job seeker—or a job strategist?

You may have felt that you were on this job search quest on your own. By now, you've gained insights to the resources, tools and knowledge that are available to you. You're not just more prepared—you're more equipped in the best way possible. No longer do you just apply and pray, you now have developed a bullish mindset for finding your internship or landing your first job after college.

Conclusion

Congratulations on reaching the end, but your adventures have just begun. As emphasized throughout this book, you are not alone in your job hunting and career preparation journey. Combine the insights gained from these chapters with your passions to make informed decisions that will help you navigate your career path. Continue acquiring new skills, developing a data-driven mindset, and refining your approach as you embark on your professional journey. With developed skills, a tailored profile, and a strong network, you will thrive.

I hope you will continue to use and refer to the sections of these chapters throughout your journey as your personal playbook. After each chapter, there is a section for you to write personal notes and actions, identify key concepts, capture quick thoughts, and apply what is relevant to you. Track your progress and learn from your experiences. Remember to leverage campus resources, even as an alum. This book provides many insights, tips, and tools from an employer perspective to help you understand what to do or avoid in maximizing your chances of finding an internship or securing your first job.

During your job search process, think of yourself as a professional "job seeker," and treat this as your full-time job. To be an effective job seeker, you need specific skills and traits. If I were to create a job description for this role, here are ten skills and traits that would make you an effective job seeker.

1. **Coachability** - An effective job seeker is constantly learning. They are continuously refining their résumé and skills. They can improve their interview style or delivery; they are proactive in getting feedback from others to improve.

2. **Empathy** - This one is a challenge to think about for a job seeker. However, empathy is a job search that requires you to think like recruiters, understanding their needs and expectations. as well as your own. It is easy to think only about yourself and the need to find a job, but be patient, be persistent, and practice empathy for others in your network.

3. **Motivation** - Just as job seekers should be coachable, they must be self-motivated to continuously learn and refine their strategies. Success in job hunting requires internal drive and perseverance to achieve goals independently.

4. **Grit** - Applying to many positions or heavily interviewing while also having companies reject you most of the time, can be quite draining. Finding a job is difficult, so you must be prepared to hustle hard. So. you need to possess the grit and determination to power through target goals, rejections, and obstacles. Keep on grinding and smiling until you win.

5. **Resourcefulness** - Job seekers who are creative in their job search and approach avoid being one-dimensional. Job seekers who think innovatively and explore diverse strategies enhance their prospects.

6. **Time Management** - Job seekers must be organized and disciplined to optimize their searches. Time management is vital for job seekers to efficiently allocate time for researching companies, following up on leads, and preparing for interviews. Balancing focused job search efforts with necessary breaks is key.

7. **Active Listening** - This is an essential skill in job hunting. A job seeker must focus on the conversation with interviewers to gather as much information as possible. You would only get details about the position from actively listening to gauge the questions being

asked or identify opportunities where you can provide solutions so that you can stand out as a candidate.

8. **Communication Skills** - While active listening is very critical, having effective communication skills (both verbal and written) is also extremely vital to a job seeker's success. Articulating qualifications effectively and responding adeptly to questions enhances a job seeker's credibility and appeal.

9. **Research Skills** - This is one that job seekers must be able to develop to stay on top of their game. You must learn to go beyond just applying to a LinkedIn post or a company career page. The more online resources you can scour for job opportunities, the more prospects you can find for yourself.

10. **Outreach Ability** - Customizing and tailoring your outreach message effectively will increase your chance of connecting with people who may be able to assist you with your job search activities. When job seekers create authentic and genuine messages, it increases the response rate and sets the stage for a more meaningful conversation. It is about moving beyond generic templates and creating a connection that resonates on a personal level.

As a parent, consultant, and practitioner, my goal is to see you succeed in your transition to the workplace, but achieving career readiness requires significant effort on your part. Simply clicking and submitting applications to job postings won't suffice. The traits and skills listed above are what I believe make an effective job seeker, but it's crucial for you to identify your strengths, acknowledge your weaknesses, and determine which traits resonate most with you.

Armed with this newfound knowledge, my aim is for you to feel empowered, increase your self-confidence, and chart a path of continuous learning to build a strong foundation for your career readiness. Equipped with these expanded skills, you're now better prepared to pursue your desired profession. Understanding the job search process from a recruiter's perspective is invaluable—something I wish I had as a guide during my own college years, as it would have led me to more deliberate decisions.

Just as I advise my college son, I hope you can leverage these tips and tools to forge ahead and accelerate your career path. I want to take a moment to express my gratitude for your time and energy spent reading this book. As a college student, I know you are incredibly busy, so I appreciate your willingness to explore these methods to improve your job search efforts. I sincerely hope you find valuable insights in this book that resonate with your journey.

If you wish to reach out to me directly for further coaching, to share your unique story, or just to give a shout-out, please send me a request to connect on LinkedIn **https://www.linkedin.com/in/edwardavila/**. Please do not just send me a blank connection request if you want me to respond (see **Chapter 10** as a reminder). Send a personal note with a *#BeBullish* hashtag. I would love to hear from you.

Lastly, I hope this book empowers you be more bullish as you successfully leap from the classroom to the workplace.

What Now?

- Pick one chapter that resonated with you and re-read it this week.
- Update your résumé or LinkedIn profile based on something new you learned.
- Reach out to a professor, advisor, or alumni for a conversation.
- Apply to one job or internship—even if it feels like a stretch.

Don't let the momentum fade. Take the first step today. You're ready.

Be bold. Be intentional. Be Bullish.

— Edward

Acknowledgments

I extend my deepest gratitude to my wife, Mylene, for all the love and care you have shown me. You have been my #1 supporter since the day we met. I appreciate you listening and providing honest opinions when I shared my work-related stories. You were by my side before *Be Bullish 101* was even a thought. There is no one else with whom I would rather stumble through life than you. I love you always and forever.

A pivotal moment in the genesis of *Be Bullish 101* occurred during an exchange with a LMU mother at a Family Weekend Event. Following my participation in a parent panel discussion on navigating the professional landscape, she approached me with words that ignited a revelation within me. 'I liked what you said on stage. You should write a book about job search strategies from an employer's perspective,' she remarked. This encounter became my 'Aha!' moment, catalyzing the commencement of this book project and finally putting pen to paper and writing it.

The foundation of *Be Bullish 101* is rooted in the experiences and endeavors of my son, Nicolas. I'm grateful you allowed me to be at your side during your four years of college. Though I'm sure there were eye-rolling moments during our discussions on job searches, I'm hopeful that you recognize the strategies and tactics in this book as you put them into practice, yielding results by landing three summer internships during your undergraduate studies. Thank you for making learning exciting and engaging when we worked together. As you leap into the working world, these experiences have established a solid foundation for you. Wherever your career takes you, I know you will do it with confidence and intention.

Writing *Be Bullish 101* would not have been possible without the support of my network throughout my professional journey. This book is the product of many learnings and collaborations from my former bosses, leaders, and mentors, with whom I have had the pleasure of working and who have significantly impacted my career. Thank you to Dr. Kimberly Cuff, Randy McMills, Gale Rothwell, Edyta Jakubek, Susan Mustacchio, Peter Kleij, Carla Mahieu, Judee Williams, Jim Wright, Diane Karija, Vern Kelley, Karen Gaydon, Joy Wolken, and Catherine Fitzsimmons. Your trust and confidence in my abilities mean the world to me. This book serves as a mirror reflecting the lasting impressions you all have made on me.

Numerous individuals contributed to the evolution of this manuscript. While acknowledging everyone is impossible, I must appreciate those whose guidance, suggestions, and feedback refined its essence. Sonia Terra, Raj Singh, Marlene Rivera, Katie Savoca, and Tania Diaz —your steadfast support, time, and contributions have been invaluable.

A debt of gratitude is owed to the remarkable educators who took a chance on a mischievous kid and shaped my journey through my early school years. To Shane Martin, Steve Artiga, Sharon Pardini, and Margorie Bennett, I am forever thankful for nurturing my love for challenges.

Last but not least, I wish to express gratitude to the often-unsung heroes—the Career Center Counselors and staff members at universities—who tirelessly guide students towards fulfilling careers. Your dedication to shaping futures does not go unnoticed.

Let's Be Bullish.

About The Author

Edward Avila is a Talent Acquisition Executive who has spent over three decades in Silicon Valley focused on building teams and organizations for high-tech companies.

In his first book, *"Be Bullish 101,"* Edward uses his corporate experience as an in-house Talent Acquisition Executive to provide insider strategies for college students and early career professionals to achieve career readiness, disrupting traditional methods of embarking on their career journey.

With 30 years of experience building global, high-performing teams that embrace innovation through data and technology, Edward has a proven track record in high-tech recruiting, executive coaching, organizational development, employer branding, and strategic workforce planning in startup and corporate environments.

Edward holds a Master's in Organizational Development from the *University of San Francisco* and a Bachelor's in Political Science from Loyola Marymount University.

Key Visual Tools Index

Figure	Title	Chapter	Purpose
1.1	Available Resources	Chapter 1	Highlights the career resources available at your university.
2.1	360-degree assessment tool	Chapter 2	Enables you to gather feedback from mentors, peers, and close connections.
3.2	Example: Backwards Planning Tool	Chapter 3	A roadmap to help you outline specific actions for career readiness.
3.3	Template: Backwards Planning Tool	Chapter 3	A blank template for building your personal career readiness plan.
4.1	Example: Career Readiness Action Plan	Chapter 4	Helps you refine your career interests, goals, and steps forward.
6.1	Impact of Automation Matrix	Chapter 6	Illustrates how automation impacts roles across different quadrants.
6.2	Example: Data Drive Action Plan	Chapter 6	Demonstrates how to use data and insights to strengthen your job strategy.
6.3	Example: Data-Driven Tracker	Chapter 6	A sample format to help you track your job search activities.
6.4	Visual Job Search Dashboard	Chapter 6	A visual display of job search progress using your tracker.

Figure	Title	Chapter	Purpose
7.1	Internship Program Calendar	Chapter 7	A month-by-month view of internship hiring cycles and planning activities.
7.2	Four Stages of Career Readiness	Chapter 7	Outlines the four developmental stages of early career preparation.
7.3	Four-Year Career Readiness Worksheet	Chapter 7	Helps map key career development milestones by year in college.
8.1	Candidate Evaluation Scorecard	Chapter 8	A rubric used by interviewers to assess core skills and competencies.
9.1	Anatomy of a LinkedIn Profile	Chapter 9	A breakdown of what a LinkedIn profile entails.
9.2	LinkedIn Recruiter	Chapter 9	Breaks down essential components of a strong LinkedIn profile.
9.3	LinkedIn Recruiter: Search Filters	Chapter 9	Displays advanced filters used by recruiters to find talent on LinkedIn.
10.1	LinkedIn Invitation Note	Chapter 10	Shows how to customize your connection requests to stand out.
11.1	S.O.A.R. Framework	Chapter 11	Shows the recruiter's view when sourcing candidates using LinkedIn tools.
11.2	S.O.A.R Storytelling Worksheet	Chapter 11	A storytelling method to structure impactful interview responses.

Figure	Title	Chapter	Purpose
12.1	Bullish Career Canvas™	Chapter 12	A strategic tool to build an actionable job search and career plan.
13.1	Interview Preparation Framework	Chapter 13	A timeline-based guide to help you prepare for interviews effectively.
13.2	Example of an Interview Process	Chapter 13	Offers a sample of what a modern interview process may include.

In Loving Memory

Fr. Robert J. ("Tex") Welch, SJ

1929-2022

Endnotes

[1] The Britannica Dictionary.

Introduction:

[2] Intelligent.com. (August 30, 2023). "4 in 10 Business Leaders Say Recent College Grads Are Unprepared To Enter Workforce".

[3] Christ, Ginger. (November 20, 2023). "Work Experience, Not College, Prepared Employees For Jobs, Study Finds", *Higher Ed Dive*.

Chapter 1:

[4] CollegeData. (2023). "Transition to College" Survey.

[5] Carr, Chloe. (August 14, 2023). "Journey of Self-Discovery In University: Finding Your Passions & Purpose", *Universal Student Living*.

[6] LeBlanc, Nicole J, MA and Marques, Luana, PhD. (August 27, 2019). "Anxiety in college: What we know and how to cope", *Harvard Health Blog*.

Chapter 2:

[7] Jobs, Steve. (June 12, 2005). "2005 Commencement Address", *Stanford News*.

[8] Eurich, Tash. (January 4, 2018). "What Self-Awareness Really Is (and How to Cultivate it), *Harvard Business Review*.

[9] Gallup (2014). "Great Jobs, Great Lives: The 2014 Gallup-Purdue Index Report". Washington DC.

[10] CollegeData (2020), "Being Involved In College: How Can It Benefit Me?".

Chapter 3:

[11] MacKay, Jory. (October 27, 2017). "This New Study Shows That People Who Think Backwards' Are More Successful". *Inc.com*.

[12] Kesty, Sarah. (May 9, 2023). "4 Ways To Teach Students Backward Planning", *Edutopia*.

Chapter 4:

[13] Flaherty, Colleen. (November 30, 2023). "Students Sound Off on Career Centers". *Inside Higher Ed.*

[14] Gurchiek, Kath. (March 31, 2022), "Study Finds Students Are Confused About How To Prepare For Their Careers". *Society for Human Resources Management.*

[15] Castro, Greg. (June 30, 2023). "How To Use ChatGPT In Your Job Search". *Indeed.*

[16] LinkedIn Opportunity Index 2000.

Chapter 5:

[17] Lammers, William, J. (March 24, 2017). "Why Don't They Ask Us For Help?". *Faculty Focus.*

[18] Kim, Y. K., & Lundberg, C. A. (2016). A structural model of the relationship between student–faculty interaction and cognitive skills development among college students. *Research in Higher Education, 57*(3), 288–309.

[19] Wikipedia, "Jerry Brown".

[20] Wikipedia, "John Vasconellos".

[21] Wikipedia, "Tom Bradley (mayor)".

[22] Wikipedia, "Gloria Molina".

[23] Edwards, Bob (February 20, 1991). "GLORIA MOLINA BECOMES NEW LA SUPERVISOR". National Public Radio.

Chapter 6:

[24] Becker, Sam. (June 21, 2023). "Applying for Jobs and Not Hearing Back? Indeed Wants to Boost Your Search, Netflix Style". *Fast Company.*

[25] Smith, Jacquelyn. (April 17, 2013). "7 Things You Probably Didn't Know About Your Job Search". *Forbes.*

[26] Myers, Sydney. (October 2, 2023). "2023 Applicant Tracking System (ATS) Usage Report: Key Shifts and Strategies for Job Seekers". *Jobscan.*

[27] Saratoga Workforce Index, *PwC.com.*

[28] Maurer, Roy. (June 23, 2017). "Employee Referrals Remain Top Source for Hires". *Society for Human Resources Management.*

[29] "2023 NACE Recruiting Benchmarks Report & Dashboard", *National Association of Colleges and Employers.*

Chapter 8:

[30] Lovich, Deborah. (October 4, 2023). "Is The War For Talent Over? If So, Who Won?" *Forbes.*

[31] Torres, Christina. (May 15, 2022). "Skills and Competencies: What's The Difference". *Degreed Blog.*

[32] Friedman, Isaac A. (June 3, 2020). "The Competent School Principal: Personality Traits and Professional Skills". *Psychology*, 11, 823-844.

Chapter 9:

[33] Prescott, Lee Ann. (October 2, 2023). "28 Recruiting Statistics On The Candidate Experience". *SmartTA Partners Blog.*

[34] LinkedIn Corporation Communications, 2017.

[35] Schawbel, D., Angulo, R. (April 22, 2013). "The Student Employment Study". *Millennial Branding.*

[36] Recruitment Success Academy, December 8, 2023.

[37] Osman, Maddy. (March 29, 2024). "Mind-Blowing LinkedIn Statistics and Facts". *Kinsta.*

[38] About LinkedIn (2024).

[39] The Aldler Group, LinkedIn's 2017 Global Recruiting Trends Report.

Chapter 10:

[40] Alder, Lou. (February 28, 2016). LinkedIn Survey.

[41] Santa Clara Valley Historical Association. (2011, October 31). *Steve Jobs on Failure* [Video]. YouTube.

Chapter 11:

[42] Villegas, Dino PhD. (July 19, 2021). "Why You Should Use Storytelling In Your Next Job Interview". Medium.

[43] Mayhew, Ruth. (March 21, 2022). "The SOAR Interview Process". *CHRON.*

Chapter 12:

[44] Mullen, Steve. (June 17 2016). "An Introduction to Lean Canvas". *Medium.*

Chapter 13:

[45] Forst, Ismirelda. (August 30, 2023). "Turning Rejection Into Opportunity: Mastering Rejection Feedback". *RecruitingDaily.com.*

[46] Mok, Aaron. (July 5, 2023). "How Long Does It Take To Get Hired In 2023?". Business Insider.

[47] Wikipedia, "Monopoly".